S E A
GOTHS
UNTIL A.D. 275
HUN TRIBES
COMBINE UNDER
ATTILA A.D. 450
OSTROGOTHS
AFTER A.D. 275
VISIGOTHS
AFTER A.D. 275
CROSS
DANUBE
A.D. 376
CROSS
DANUBE
A.D. 377
BLACK SEA
SETTLE
A.D. 378-395
ADRIANOPLE
A.D. 378
N E A N
The
GREAT
MIGRATIONS

DARK AGE WARRIOR

By the same author

A KNIGHT AND HIS ARMOUR

A KNIGHT AND HIS HORSE

A KNIGHT AND HIS WEAPONS

A KNIGHT AND HIS CASTLE

A KNIGHT IN BATTLE

THE SWORD IN THE AGE OF CHIVALRY

THE ARCHAEOLOGY OF WEAPONS

DARK AGE WARRIOR

EWART OAKESHOTT
F.S.A.

Illustrated by the author

LUTTERWORTH PRESS
GUILDFORD AND LONDON

First published 1974

ACKNOWLEDGEMENT

The extract from *Beowulf* which appears on page 28 is taken from Beowulf: The Oldest English Epic, translated by Charles W. Kennedy, copyright 1940 by Oxford University Press Inc., reprinted by kind permission.

ISBN 0 7188 2079 7

Printed in Great Britain photolitho
by Ebenezer Baylis and Son, Limited,
The Trinity Press, Worcester and London

CONTENTS

INTRODUCTION

INVASION, MIGRATION AND SETTLEMENT

One of the richest and most magnificent archaeological treasures ever to be found was discovered in Suffolk, England, in 1939, near the coast at the mouth of the little River Deben at a place called Sutton Hoo. Here, nearly fourteen hundred years ago, a king's property was buried in his great longship. There was a hoard of marvellous jewellery, a lot of fine silver table-ware, the king's drinking-horns, his harp, his war-standard and his war-gear decorated with gold, silver and jewels.

The fact that this stuff was found in England is important (you can see it in London in the British Museum), but far more important, and more interesting, is the royal burial itself—more puzzling, too; for though it was the grave of a monarch, stuffed with treasure, there was no body in it! Just the treasure and the weapons of a king who wasn't there!

This book is not about the treasure, or the East Anglian royal family who once owned it, or even the Anglo-Saxon people who lived in England at the time it was buried. It is about the time itself, the long period during which the Anglo-Saxons gradually turned the Roman province of Britannia into a land named after them, England. But the Anglo-Saxon conquest and settlement of Britain was only an isolated and not very important event in a huge series of invasions, wars, migrations and settlements which surged to-and-fro across Europe for four hundred years, four desperate centuries in which the age-old, settled pattern of the Roman Empire was destroyed and out of which, in the end, came the Europe of today.

The folk who were living in England when the longship was buried at Sutton Hoo had already been there for a long time. They had begun to arrive some three hundred years before, boatload by boatload, appearing out of the cold wastes of the North Sea. They had landed on the beaches, camped for a while near the shore, then pushed inland to carve little homesteads for themselves out of the thick forest and scrubland. Many groups had been met by the native Britons, who either killed them all, or killed the warriors and took the women and children for slaves.

This, of course, is exactly what happened on the east coasts of America more than a thousand years after. When the English, French and Dutch settlers began to carve out places for them-

selves, they had to take the land they got from the Indian tribes. Sometimes they were successful, sometimes not; and if not, then they were killed or enslaved. So it was when the Saxons came to Britain.

The Saxons were a Teutonic people, while the Britons were Celtic; but because Britain was a province of the Roman Empire, the native people are generally called Romano-Britons.

Now, what does all this mean? Teutons, Celts, Romans—who were they? Where did they live? At the height of the Roman Empire, all of Europe, and a good deal of Western Asia, was peopled by these three races. The Teutons and Celts were divided into many tribes, large and small, while the Romans were like the Americans or Russians today, a Super-Power which ruled a great part of the world.

The wielders of this power were called Romans because their base, the centre from which all this great Empire was ruled, was a city called Rome. They were not all citizens of Rome of course; they were Italians and Etruscans and Greeks and Africans, but because Rome was the hub of the world, they were all known as Romans.

These Romans started away back in the mists of the past, a tough little tribe of farmer-soldiers living in central Italy. Some seven hundred years before the birth of Christ, they built themselves a town and called it 'Roma'. They were hard-working folk, and efficient. They knew how to organise themselves and other people, and they were very good at soldiering. Soon they had soldiered their way through Italy, and conquered everyone else who lived there. Then they went on, expanding and widening their power, until they ruled very nearly all the world—that is, those parts of the world that were known to them, which by our standards was precious little.

If you were to look at a map of America in the time of the Pilgrim Fathers, about A.D. 1620, you'd see the same thing—a vast mass of territory which was peopled only by the nations and tribes of the Indians, a great area quite unknown to the coastal settlers, except of course what they could learn about it from the tales which they heard from Indian traders. That's what Europe was like at the time of the Sutton Hoo Burial, about A.D. 650.

What do we mean by 'A.D.' and 'B.C.' when we are using historical dating? If you try to understand historical happenings without dates, all you get is a lot of jumbled evidence without order. Now, all dating has to have a starting point. The peoples of Europe have for nearly two thousand years used the Christian method of dating, starting with the year in which Christ was born. This method has, of course, spread to a great many parts of the modern world where Europeans settled and colonised—like America, Australia, New Zealand, India, and so on. The year in which I am writing this is A.D. 1973—that is, one thousand nine hundred and seventy-three years after the year of Christ's birth—and the 'A.D.' represents the initial letters of the Latin words, *Anno Domini*, which means 'Year of the Lord'. When the Christians first started using this method of dating, they named each year for the most tremendous event which, in their opinion, had ever happened; they would write or say, in effect, 'In this three hundred and seventy-sixth year of Our Lord', as if it referred to his age—which of course it did. The Christians considered that Christ rose from the dead, so to speak of his 376th year—or his 1973rd—is quite sensible.

Then what about 'B.C.'? The English-speaking world uses it—it simply means 'Before Christ' (the A.D. system in reverse), but most other Europeans use the initials 'A.C.' for the old Latin phrase *Ante Christus* which means exactly the same thing.

The ancient Romans dated history from the year of the foundation of Rome—to them *this* was the most tremendous event in their history. The Jews used, and still do, another system; their dating starts with the time when, in their opinion, the world was created—3761 B.C., giving them the most ancient and unbroken system of all. The Muslims count time from what they call the Hegira—the day when the Prophet Muhammed fled from Mecca to Medina—A.D. 622 in Christian dating. And so on.

So, the Sutton Hoo ship was buried in its mound at some time around A.D. 675, when these Teutonic Anglian folk had been coming in small raiding parties to this island for about four hundred years, and had driven the native British back and settled in it for more than two hundred years. The map at the very front of this book shows their sea-routes. They were only able to settle in Britain because the power of the Romans had become very weak during the fourth century—that is, the hundred years between A.D. 300 and A.D. 400—and in 410 the last Roman soldiers were withdrawn from Britain; this left the people nearly defenceless, because for over four hundred years they had relied upon strong Roman 'armies of occupation' to defend them; and although the Britons were, as individuals, great fighters, and although they were quite good at small gang-fights and little tribal wars among themselves, they were quite incapable of banding together to fight the Teutonic Angles and Saxons who were, on the whole, better fighters;

they were stubborn and obstinate too, like their modern descendants, and went on fighting when they were dog-tired, hungry, discouraged and sick, and when it looked to all common-sense as if they were beaten. The Celtic Britons were like *their* descendants, the Welsh, the Irish and the Highland Scots. Tremendously brave and fiery in battle, they lost heart too soon, and tended to stop fighting when an extra few hours or days of sticking it out would have given them victory.

Except, that is, for one space of time when they did stick it out and band together, perhaps fifty years between about A.D. 480 and 530. Then the British more or less united under a great war-leader; not a king, nor a tribal chief, but a war-leader who by the force of his personality was able to weld the tribes together to resist and turn back the Teutonic invaders. He was a Romano-British nobleman named Artorius; the Celts called him Arthur—Arthur Amheradwr, Arthur the Emperor. He has become a great national hero in England, for though he was British, and fought the Saxons and Angles tooth and nail, he changed the course of English history. Because of him, the Britons withstood, and for a time actually *beat*, the alien people who sought to steal their homeland. And they did it alone, without any help from the failing power of Rome.

At this time, *because* the Roman power was failing, the whole of Europe—indeed, almost the whole world—was overrun by Teutonic invaders. And nobody else stood up to them as the British did. The Romans did their best to defend their provinces, but the provincial Celtic peoples in Gaul and Italy and Spain did little to defend themselves.

To English people this conquest of Britain by the Angles and Saxons is, naturally, very important. All the same, it was only a very small part of the great series of movements which spread over the whole of Europe for centuries, and which we call the Great Migrations. (This is illustrated in the map at the very front of this book.) The elaborate, civilised structure of the Roman Empire was broken to pieces, and the map was changed completely. But out of a welter of barbarism, the nations of modern Europe finally grew.

The century in which Christ was born saw the beginnings of these fearful changes which were to overthrow the ancient world. Take the hundred years 50 B.C. to A.D. 50: at the start of this period, the ancient world was still much the same as it had been for the previous two thousand years. In 50 B.C. it was something like this:

The Mediterranean and a lot of the Middle East had come under Roman rule, so had most of North Africa. The civilisation of ancient Greece was still active, though Greece itself was a Roman province. The three-thousand-year-old civilisation of Egypt was in the last stages of its old age, and was soon in its turn to become a province of the Roman Empire. Persia, which now more or less included ancient Babylonia and Assyria, was still a mighty power and was to grow far greater.

To the northward of the Mediterranean countries were the vast, more or less unknown, lands of Central Europe, and the mysterious islands of Britannia and Hibernia. These lands were peopled by Celtic tribes, who were warlike and highly civilised; and though they had no kind of central government, they were none the less part of a sort of Celtic 'Empire', very much to be reckoned with, and the lands of Gaul (modern France) and Helvetia (modern Switzerland) were the heart of it. Further north still, and to the eastward, along the Rhine and the

Danube, dwelt the Teutonic tribes of Germany, savage, aggressive and mysterious. To the north and east again, cut off from the Old World by the vast black forests and marshes of Germany, were other peoples of whom Rome knew nothing—though in four centuries' time the Romans were to know their descendants far too well. They were the Vandals and the Goths, Longobards, Saxons, Angles, Jutes, and Danes. These were the folk who swept away the Celts and the Roman Empire and formed the basis of modern Europe. By the end of this hundred years—by A.D. 50—the process of change had begun.

Only a few of these peoples seem to have anything to do with English history, so why should we be concerned with the others? Because, of course, what they did, and where they went, had indeed a profound effect on English history; to leave them out and just learn about the Angles and Saxons and Jutes is like studying modern history without taking America or Australia or Japan into account. All the same, we don't often hear anything about them. Their names are connected in our minds only with things seeming to have nothing at all to do with the Great Migrations of the fifth and sixth centuries. To us, a Vandal is a hooligan who breaks up telephone kiosks and such; Gothic is a type of church-architecture; and the name Lombard is associated with banking. Why?

The word 'Vandal' began to be used late in the eighteenth century to denote a breaker-up of things. This was because at that period, one of the most cultured and civilised the world has known, all things Greek and Roman were looked upon as terribly important and precious. To the scholars and historians who studied classical—that is, Greek or Roman—life and literature, Vandals and Goths were the End. They were the people above all others (they thought) who had broken up and scattered that ancient and precious civilisation. So they began to use the word Vandal to mean any hooligan who destroyed things. And because they regarded classical art and architecture as the only kind worth thinking about, they began to refer to the medieval styles of painting, sculpture, and particularly building as 'Gothic'.

Then, what about Lombard Banking? Well, the Longobards eventually settled in Northern Italy, and their name got shortened to Lombard; during the Middle Ages (the period from about A.D. 500-1500) the business men of the Lombard cities, particularly Florence, grew very rich and became bankers to the rest of the Western world. So much so that they had their own special quarters in Europe's great cities—there is still a street called Lombard Street in London—and their name became firmly associated with banking.

All these Germanic folk belonged to different groups with different tribal names, but really they were all of the same race—the same ethnic group, if you like to put it that way. For convenience, we can break the Teutonic race down into two main sections, the Germans and the Scandinavians. Of the two, the Germans were the more primitive and savage, the Scandinavians the more civilised, better organised, and in the end, far more terrible. In the German section there were very many tribes. In the Scandinavian section there were Goths, Vandals, Longobards, Danes, Norse, Jutes, Angles and Burgundians. Now here is one group left right out. What about the Saxons?

They were almost a race on their own, together with their neighbours the Frisians, living between the Germans to the west and south and the Scandinavians to the north and east. Their culture—that is, their art and their poetry, as it showed itself once they had settled down in Britain—is closer to the Scandinavian than to the German; in fact, the Germans of this period, up to about the sixth century, *had* no art (as we know it) and no culture. Their only trade, their only sport, their only art, was war; their only craft the making of weapons. They scared the Romans to death, and no wonder.

To make it easier to understand history, we divide it up into conveniently labelled chunks, or periods. We have The Roman Period (roughly B.C. 700–A.D. 650), The Migration Period (roughly A.D. 300–800), and The Viking Period (roughly A.D. 750–1050). These are sub-divisions of the larger chunks which we call Ages—Stone Age, Bronze Age, Iron Age. Into the Iron Age come our first two Periods: the Roman Period is often called The Roman Iron Age, the Migration Period The Teutonic Iron Age, with a Celtic Iron Age sandwiched between them and overlapping both. Then, after The Teutonic Iron Age we have The Middle Ages—Early, Central and Late. And, to add still more to your confusion, the time between A.D. 350 and about 800 is very often called The Dark Ages. Dark, because the time was bloody and chaotic, but more because up to seventy or eighty years ago, historians knew practically nothing about it, and it was dark indeed. But thanks to modern historical research, and to modern archaeological discoveries, the light is brightening all the time, and the Dark Ages are really dark no longer.

But to people who had to live through them—and they lasted four hundred and fifty years: over fifteen generations! —they were hideously dark. Even so, here and there in Gaul and Helvetia and Britain and Italy and Greece, little groups of people survived to resist the spread of barbarism. Not groups of fighting men, but of scholars and artists. And of all the European countries swamped by the barbarians, one missed the invasions altogether, and stood out as a centre of art and learning. This was the island of Hibernia, now known as Ireland.

The effect of these resisting groups was infectious like measles. They were civilised and more or less comfortable, and they made and loved beautiful things: and it was catching. The barbarians, wherever they came up against it, did catch it; and just like measles, it spread. And spread, until in the end almost everyone everywhere had caught it; and the tide of barbarity was turned back. Once people had this wish to be civilised, they had to have a home of some sort to be civilised *in*—better and more lasting than a covered wagon or a tent or a hut. By about A.D. 700 the folk-wanderings shown in the map had stopped, and the nations had settled into new homes and adopted a better way of life. After all, it was three hundred years since the Migrations had begun! But just when things did seem to be settling down, it was all threatened again from the outside, this time by a fierce warrior race of religious fanatics—the Arabic peoples of North Africa with their new, intense Muslim faith. They frightened Teutonic Europe as much as once the Teutons had frightened Roman Europe. There was half-a-century or so of fierce fighting, and the tide of Islam (which means 'submission to the will of God') was turned back. But the threat had done a great deal to steady and strengthen the still rather frail civilisation of Europe.

Then, thanks to the strength and genius of a single man, all these trends towards civilisation were linked together, and

B

the new pattern, which was to endure for over a thousand years, took shape. The man was Charles, King of the Franks, who ever since his death in A.D. 814 has been known as Charlemagne or Charles the Great. He was the European counterpart of our own Arthur; but Arthur's work was swept away, while Charlemagne's remains to this day.

He was a great ruler in every way, a great statesman, a great soldier, a great administrator, and it was an extraordinary piece of luck for Europe and the world that he was born the son of the King of the Franks, for only by being a monarch could he have done what he did. Over and above his political force, however, he had one enormous gift—he believed passionately in the value of civilisation—of Order, and Art, and above everything, the written word and the ability to read it. He ruled from A.D. 778 until 814, and in that time he sorted out, organised and welded into a political whole all the contesting and squabbling peoples of Europe. The Dark Ages were over, and a unified Europe moved forward towards the greatness of the Middle Ages.

The arms used by the 'Wandering Folk' of the Dark Ages were quite different from those of the Romans, who had simply copied or adapted the armour and weapons of the Ancient Greeks, who had based theirs upon what had been used in Ancient Egypt, Persia and Assyria. The Celtic and Teutonic barbarians of the north had invented and developed their own forms of sword, spear and axe. While Greeks and Romans had followed the old Bronze Age patterns, the Celts, who in about 500 B.C. had been the first to discover the practical possibilities of using forged iron to make large weapons, made effective use of their smithing skills, as we shall see.

Of all the 'Barbarian' folk, the Scandinavians were the most given to making and telling great yarns about their weapons and their feats of arms. Very few of these tales survive from the Longobards or the Goths or the Vandals because as races they were absorbed by the illiterate Franks or dispersed, but the Northmen who stayed at home in the heartlands of Sweden and Norway and Denmark continued to flourish as highly individual peoples, and spread all over North-Western Europe. Among them of course were the Saxons and the Danes and the Normans, the particular ancestors of modern Great Britain. They all survived to tell their tales, and richly dramatic tales they were.

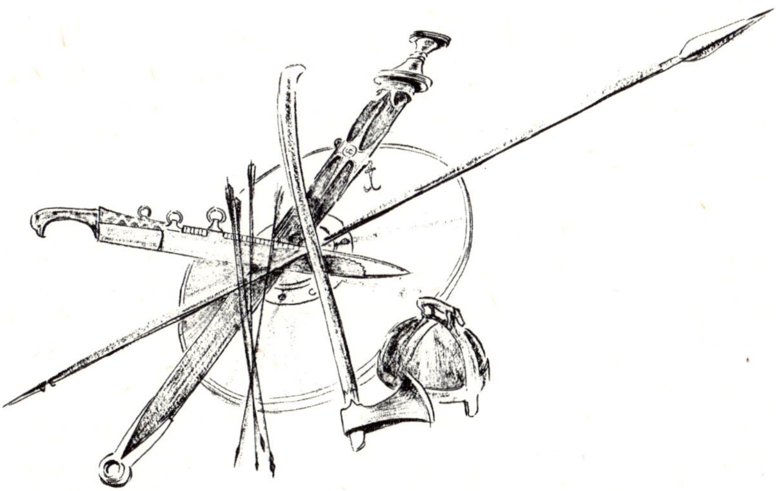

CHAPTER I

POET, HISTORIAN AND ARCHAEOLOGIST

WEAPONS always had a very special place in the old tales told by the peoples of the north, the Vikings and their forebears. They were always spoken of with respect; the sword in particular was regarded as much more than a mere instrument of aggression and self-preservation; it was the special symbol of the warrior, part of his fighting spirit as well as his shoulder-companion. Swords were considered to be the work of giants or god-like craftsmen, and often a very particularly fine sword or spear or axe would be spoken of as the work of Weland, the Smith of the Gods.

The people who lived in these northern lands were farmers, seafarers and warriors. This sounds as if there were three sorts of men, but it was not so. The farmer was a seaman as well, and if he was to survive he had to be a warrior too. Because the conditions of life were so harsh, and because there was barely enough land which could be farmed to go round, these men took to piracy as ducks take to water. Plunder from merchant ships, loot from raided towns and villages ashore, or stuff taken from a rival pirate—all such gains were considered perfectly lawful and respectable ways of making a living. Naturally enough, in these conditions pirates or raiders joined together in bands under vigorous and competent leaders, and from very early times such bands roved far afield in their search for loot. They often troubled the shores of Britain during the time of the

Roman occupation; and by the time the Romans left in A.D. 410, bands of them from the lands which are now Denmark and Holland had begun to settle in eastern and south-eastern Britain. From the countries further north, now Sweden and Norway, a few bold spirits had braved the long sea-passage across the North Sea to raid and settle in Scotland and North Britain, and during the fifth and sixth centuries, from about A.D. 400–600, more and more of them came in their long open rowing boats to make a home in this island.

It is the weapons which these people used in their raids and warrings that we are going to look at. Luckily for us, a great many of them—swords, axes, spears, bows and arrows, and knives—have been preserved in very good condition, so we can see just what they were like. Also, as I said at the beginning, these people were always telling tales in which weapons played a very important part. So when we hear their tales, listen to what they say about their weapons, and then look at the actual ones which have come down to us, we can really feel that we know something about them. As well as these two sources of information, we have a third which we can use as a sort of control. Though by the time these weapons were in use the great wide-reaching power of the Roman Empire had dwindled away and Europe was almost completely over-run with barbarians who could neither read nor write (though they *could* talk and sing and compose magnificent poetry), there were still many men who *could* write, in Latin and Greek. Some of them were interested enough in what was going on in the world around them to want to write about it all. They are called historians now, but really they were a bit like modern journalists, writing down what went on. They had a good deal to say about the weapons and fighting methods of these barbarians too; when we check their comments with the poems and sagas and with the archaeological material taken from the earth, we can piece together a very clear picture not only of what these weapons were like, but how they were used.

Before I go on to describe some of these in detail, let's just look at the three ways in which we have found out about them: the stories and poems, the work of the Latin historians, and the archaeological finds; but even before that, for the sake of clarity later on, a word about who these barbarians were and where they lived.

By about A.D. 550 all of Europe, once part of the Roman Empire, had been over-run; as I said in my Introduction, there were many different tribes, though some were quite small comprising only a few thousand folk, and were overshadowed by the larger peoples. Italy was occupied by Goths, except in the north where the Lombards settled. Spain and most of Southern France was the kingdom of the Visigoths, while northern France and part of West Germany was the land of the Franks. Belgium, Holland and South Denmark was the country of the Saxons, who at this time were in the process of moving over into Britain. Further north, in Denmark and Sweden and Norway were the lands of the Geats and Scyldings.

Many tribes, many peoples, all with different names. But they were all, as it were, cousins. They came of the same Germanic stock, spoke very similar languages and their cultures and ways of life were similar. And the weapons they used were very similar too, often so much so that we cannot say that the sword of a Geat from Jutland is any different from one used by a Longobard from Milan. This is most important to remember, for though we are going to look mainly at the weapons of our own ancestors, the Anglo-Saxons in Britain in the period following the departure of the Roman legions (A.D. 410-700), these were identical with those used elsewhere in Europe.

These people of the north were great story-tellers. Next to fighting, there was nothing they loved more than making poetry and telling tales. These, originally, were never written down, but were passed on by word of mouth for generation after generation; but if the tale or the poem was particularly good, sooner or later someone who could write would be sure to set it down, often when the tale itself was centuries old. The poem *Beowulf* is rather like this, for it had been going around for some hundred and fifty years before it was written down. By a series of chances a copy of it, made some two hundred years after the original writing, has come down to us. It is the same with some of the poems and songs, the 'Edda' poems as they are called. These were one sort of tale; another sort is what were called 'sagas', a word which in the old Norse language simply means 'tellings'. These told of the doings of certain families, chieftains and heroes, and like *Beowulf* and the Eddas were told by word of mouth until, very much later, in the thirteenth century—as much as six hundred years after the people about whom some of the tales are told were living!—many of them were written down.

In all of these literary works there are endless fascinating 'tellings' about sword and axe and spear and how they were made and used.

The Latin historians, or chroniclers, were educated men who for various reasons wrote down the events of their own times;

unlike the Norse poets, they were not always actual eye-witnesses of the things they recounted, but their descriptions of arms and fighting are of great value because of their educated ability to set down clearly what they wanted to say. So while the Norse poets give us, as it were, the soul of the weapon, the Latin writers give us a specification. The two together are most useful, but it is when both poetic soul and historical specification are applied to the examples of actual arms found in the earth that they come to life.

It is lucky for us today that the old Celtic and Germanic folk believed it to be necessary to put arms into the graves of dead warriors. Countless weapons, as well as shields and helmets and mailcoats, were laid in graves; many have been recovered, and no doubt very many more still await discovery. But these ancient warrior-folk had another strange custom which has proved to be of far greater value and interest to the archaeologists than even the grave-finds.

Here at once we are helped by two of the Latin writers I have just mentioned. One is a character you all know, though—unless you study Latin—probably not as a writer: Julius Caesar. In his 'Commentaries' about his conquest of Gaul in 57 B.C. he writes of the Romans' opponents:

> 'When they have decided to fight a battle they generally vow to Mars the booty they hope to take, and after a victory they sacrifice the captured animals and collect the rest of the spoil in one spot. Among many of the tribes, high piles of it can be seen on consecrated ground; and it is an almost unknown thing for anyone to dare, in defiance of religious law, to conceal his booty at home or to remove anything placed on the piles. Such a crime is punishable by a terrible death under torture.'

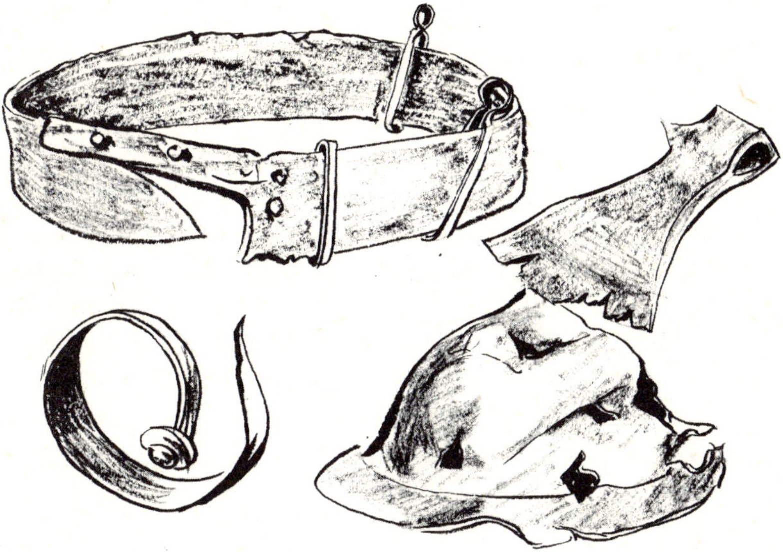

Arms destroyed before burial

Fifty years or so earlier, another historian called Orosius wrote:

> 'When the enemy had taken possession of two camps and an immense booty, they destroyed under new and strange oaths all that had fallen into their hands. The clothes were torn and thrown away, gold and silver thrown into the river, the ring-armour of the men cut to pieces, the accoutrements of the horses destroyed, the horses themselves thrown into the water, and the men with ropes around their necks suspended to the trees, so that there was no more booty for the victors than there was mercy for the conquered.'

Curiously enough, the Germanic and Celtic people who

did these things never told about them in their stories and poems; this was left to the Latin writers. But, for our purposes, they really did far better than talking about these great deposits of arms; they made them, and went on making them until nearly A.D. 500. It so happened that just about a hundred years ago, a whole series of such deposits was found and dug up in Denmark. They ranged in date from about A.D. 50 right up to about 450, and between them they contained a fantastic variety of things, naturally enough all military. And they are astonishingly well preserved, for though they were originally put into shallow lakes or meres—we know they were sunk in water because things that would float were deliberately pegged into the mud of the bottom or held down by heavy

Sword from Kragehul bog, fourth century

stones—during the seventeen or eighteen centuries between, peat has formed in the meres and they have become bogs or moorland. Now peat has chemical properties which preserve iron and wood to an astonishing degree, so when these marvellous swords and spears, shields and mailcoats, buckles, belts and jewellery were found, they were not very much perished. In one bog at Thorsbjerg there were even a couple of shirts and a pair of trousers!

It was found in these deposits that what Orosius had said was true; many of the objects had been deliberately bent up, or broken, or cut into pieces. But this deliberate damage does not in any way prevent our seeing exactly how they were made and decorated. Luckily many were not damaged, and in the National Museum at Copenhagen you can see literally dozens of splendid swords, looking much as they looked eighteen hundred years ago.

CHAPTER 2

'BRIGHT AND FIRE-HARDENED'

Then the Geats marched on. Behind, at her mooring,
Fastened at anchor, their broad-beamed boat
Safely rode at her swinging cable.
Boar-heads glittered on glistening helmets
Above their cheek-guards, gleaming with gold
Bright and fire-hardened the Boar held watch
Over the column of marching men.
Onward they hurried in eager haste
Till their eyes caught sight of a high-built hall,
Splendid with gold, the seat of a king
Most stately of structures under the sun.
The street had paving of coloured stone,
The path was plain to the marching men.
Bright were their byrnies, hard and hand-linked;
In their shining armour the ring-mail sang
As the troop in their war-gear marched to the hall.
The sea-weary sailors set down their shields,
Their wide, bright bucklers along the wall,
And sank to the bench. Their byrnies rang,
Their stout spears stood in a stack together,
Shod with iron and shaped of ash.

There is the poet, telling of Beowulf's arrival at the hall of Hrothgar, King of the Geats. This is the sort of tale our Germanic ancestors loved to hear, and you must admit it

Remains of helmet with bronze boar, from Benty Grange Farm, Derbyshire

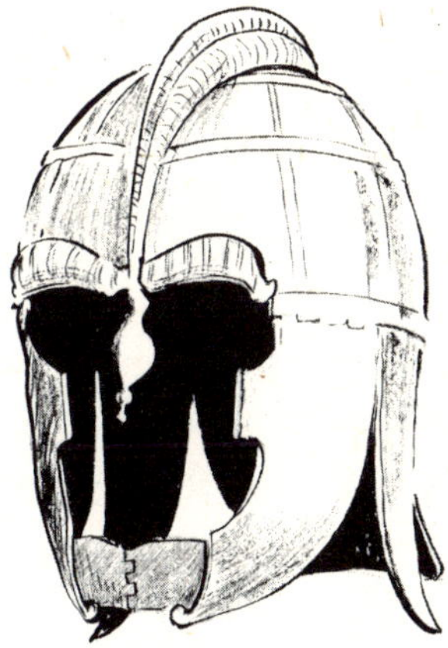

Helmet from royal grave at Valsgärde, Sweden: sixth century

sounds magnificent today. But what does it *mean*? What, for instance, can 'Bright and fire-hardened the Boar held watch' mean? Well, this is where archaeology comes in to help us. We know that from very remote times the boar was held by the folk of north-western Europe to have great protective powers. What could be more sensible, then, than to put him on top of your helmet? In fact, a few lines earlier it says so: 'Boar-heads glittered on glistening helmets, above their cheek-guards, gleaming with gold.'

If you go to the British Museum in London, you will see exactly such a helmet, while in Sweden there are several more, boar-heads, cheek-guards, gold and all. They come from the graves of kings; none have been found in the graves of lesser warriors, so we must assume that such helmets were rare and costly things. It sounds rather as though all of Beowulf's followers wore them, but then it was a picked band of princely companions he had with him. The one in the British Museum comes from the fabulously rich ship-burial of Sutton Hoo in Suffolk, and the Swedish ones come from similar burials at Vendel and Valsgärde near Uppsala, the graves of kings.

Let's have a look at some of the surviving splendid helmets. They differ a little in detail but have several points in common. All have a rounded skull, following the shape of a man's head; across the top of this skull runs a ridge-like crest, at the point of which, where it comes down between the eyes, is a stylised boar's head. There is a visor, hinged below the brow, which has apertures cut out over the eyes, with built-up eyebrows above and a nose between; there are broad flaps hanging from the sides of the skull to cover the cheeks, and another piece at the back shaped to cover the back of the neck.

These helmets were made of iron, but their surfaces were covered with small plates of thin bronze; these small plates were embossed with designs stamped into them. The Sutton Hoo helmet has a few of these fragile plates still in place. We know that the Swedish ones had them because the narrow, ribbon-like strips of bronze which held them are still there. There have also been found in Sweden a series of small bronze plaques carved in low relief with designs showing gods and warriors. It was with these and other such stamps that the thin bronze plates were embossed. Some of these plates were found in Oland in Sweden.

When new, these helmets must have looked magnificent, for the bronze plates were tinned, so that they shone like silver, and the ribbon-like strips which held them in position were gilded. The iron crests were gilded and inlaid in various

Bronze plaques for impressing helmet plates: from Torslunda, Sweden

ways with silver wires; so were the eybrows; and in the case of the Sutton Hoo helmet, which in its day was the richest of them all, the nose and close-trimmed moustache too. Under each of the silver-inlaid eyebrows of the Sutton Hoo helmet was a row of square-cut garnets let into the bronze, with similar ones outlining the mouth under the moustache. The stylised boar's head between the eyebrows—which looks more like a duck with dragon's teeth—was gilded and had eyes of inset garnets.

Inside these helmets would have been some sort of padded lining, like the lining of a modern crash helmet. They were

Helmet from royal grave at Vendel, Sweden: sixth century

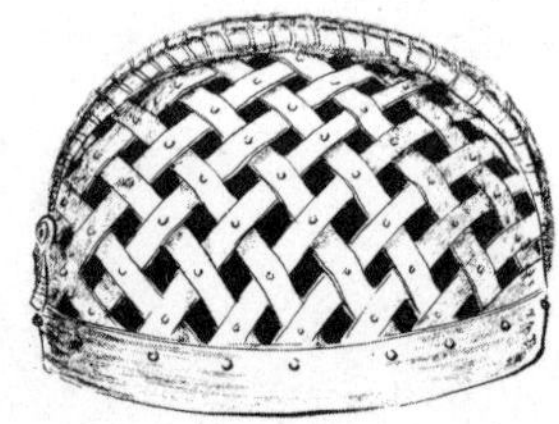

Helmet from Ultuna, Sweden

held on firmly by straps fastened to the bottom of each cheek-guard and buckled under the chin.

More ordinary warriors in these times wore much simpler helmets, generally shaped like a pea-nut, made sometimes of iron but probably more often of hardened leather. Some helmets, however, were like hats with comparatively wide brims.

There is a popular belief, with no evidence at all to support it, that all these Norse people, from the time of the Saxon invasion of this country during the fifth century to the end of the Viking age in about A.D. 1050, wore helmets with great horns or wings fastened to the sides. They did not! However, on one of the bronze plates on the Sutton Hoo helmet, and on one of the bronze relief stamps from which similar plates were made, men *are* shown wearing helmets with great curving horns on them. There are at least two actual helmets surviving, too, with horns; therefore I think we need to have some

Bronze ceremonial helmet, from Viksó, Sweden: 1500 B.C.

Bronze ceremonial helmet found in the River Thames at Battersea: A.D. 50

explanation of the whole question. Take two of the surviving horned helmets first. One is in the Swedish National Museum in Stockholm; it is beaten out of a single sheet of bronze, and has two long, slender curved horns with little knobs at their tips. But it has nothing whatever to do with the Teutonic pirates of the sixth century or the Vikings of the eighth. It comes from a period nearly *two thousand* years earlier, from the Middle Bronze age, and is a ceremonial head-dress, for the bronze it is made from is very thin and would be quite useless as a protection for any warrior's head. The second of these horned helmets is also made of bronze, but it is a finer specimen altogether and could be quite effective as a helmet. It was found in the River Thames, near Battersea in London. The helmet is small and nut-shaped, and the horns are short and straight, very thick where they spring from the skull of the helmet and tapering to blunt, sort of cut-off points. This too has nothing to do with the Vikings, for it is Celtic and dates from about the time of Julius Caesar's invasion of Britain in 55 B.C. It too, though suitable for wearing in battle, is probably a chief's helmet.

What about the horned helmets shown on the sixth century helmet-plate and relief stamp, then? Well, in both cases these are worn by either gods or priests. From very remote times—at least from the time of the cave-dwelling palaeolithic hunting folk—bulls' horns or stags' antlers were worn on the heads of priests, or Shamans or witch-doctors as they are called in present-day primitive cultures. The Red Indians' Shamans wore horns, so do many witch-doctors in Africa.

But no fighting man with a grain of commonsense would lumber himself with a pair of horns spreading out of his helmet. Just think about it for a moment. Imagine you are in the thick of a fight, with sword- and axe-blows whistling around your head. The first one to strike one of the horns on your helmet, even a light glancing blow, would send it spinning off, or would smash it down on one side so that its lower rim clawed your ear off. No, I'm afraid all those horned helmets worn by terribly ferocious and romantic-looking warriors you are constantly reading about, or seeing pictures of, are, historically speaking, so much romantic rubbish. The tribal or family Shaman would wear one, true enough, at a feast or a funeral or a wedding, or even in a battle, but he'd take very good care not to get mixed up in the fighting.

There are not many pictures of warriors which were drawn or painted or sculpted during the times we are talking about, but there are a few. Certainly enough to show us that men fought in sensible little nut-shaped or hat-shaped helmets and not horned ones. A good example of one such helmet is from a

Stone, carved in bas-relief, with warriors: ninth century

Frankish grave of about A.D. 650. It is as rich as the Norse ones, but of a plain nut-shape. It seems that only the Swedes produced very rich and elaborate helmets like the Sutton Hoo one. Most of the other peoples in this period—Franks, Goths, Longobards and Vandals—wore the ordinary kind, with or without cheek-guards.

The next item of war-gear we find in this passage of *Beowulf* gives you a clue to its meaning: 'Bright were their byrnies, hard and hand-linked.' You will probably guess right away that the poet means their mail shirts; things like knitted jerseys, made not of wool but of thousands of little hand-forged iron rings all linked together, forming a material known to us as mail. Nearly always, unfortunately, called 'chain-mail' today, though it has only been called that since about 1760. The Saxons and Vikings had no special word for the stuff itself, though the shirts they made from it they called 'byrnies'. They always used poetic expressions, such as 'Net of the Spears' or 'Odin's Web' or 'War-net, woven by cunning of smith'. All net names; quite right, for it was in fact, a very close-meshed net. The diagram of a bit of mail on page 41 shows you how the rings are linked together.

Then why is it called 'mail'? This has become an English word, but it went through many stages before it came into our language, like this: the Romans used the stuff (indeed their Celtic enemies, the Gauls, had been using it for centuries before they did) and they called it, simply, 'net'—*macula*—a Latin word meaning dots or spots. Because a net looks rather like a lot of dots joined together, they didn't bother to have a different word for it; they just called it '*macula*'; and, always economical, they applied this word to any sort of net, including

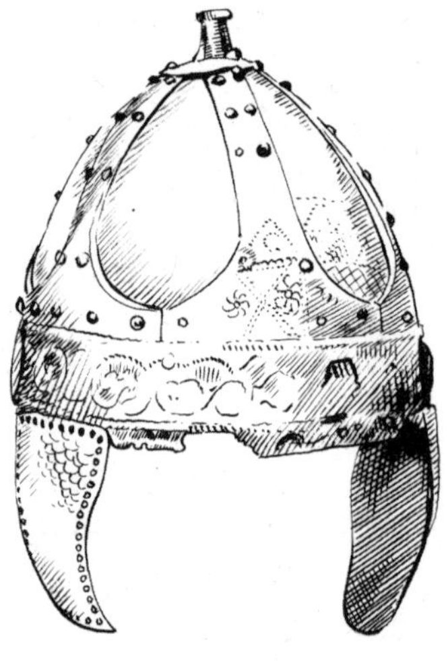

This helmet, of a severely practical shape, was found in the grave of a chieftain at Morken in Germany, dating from about A.D. 650. It is made of the same materials as the Vendel helmet (page 32) and the Sutton Hoo helmet, but is of a shape which had been in use since the Bronze Age and was to continue as the most practical form of helmet until the fifteenth century A.D. The ancient Persians and the Assyrians used exactly the same form of helmet too, constructed in the same way.

the war-net. In the course of time, this word crept into the languages which were developing from the mixture of Latin and barbarian races—French and Italian. But it changed from *macula* to *maglia* in Italian and *mailles* in French. The French version was brought into England with the Norman conquerors after 1066, and when the English had got hold of *mailles* they pronounced it rather as it was spelt, as 'mail'. But all this took a very long time. There is no evidence for the word 'mail' being used in English until the thirteenth century. Be that as it may, the war-net of Beowulf became *maglia*, *mailles* and mail; never, never, chain-mail until long after this type of armour had ceased to be used.

The making of mail was a complicated process which cannot be described here in detail, but I can give you a general idea of how it was done. There were two main processes: the making of the rings and the linking of them together to make the garment. The rings started as lengths of wire. (Incidentally the art of wire-drawing was obviously known to the pre-Roman Celts). To make a number of rings you wind your length of wire tightly round a piece of rod of the diameter you want. This gives you a tight, long coil of wire. Then you cut through the entire coil along the top; this separates it into as many open rings as there are loops in the coil. The two ends of each ring are swaged—flattened out—and a hole is punched in each flattened end. The rings are now ready for riveting into a mesh. The rivets are tiny pieces of soft iron, wedge-shaped.

The actual garment of mail is put together in exactly the same way as a pullover is knitted. The rings are linked in rows; where the garment widens, the number of rings is increased; and where it narrows, decreased. The mail-maker

Embossed silver bowl found in Hungary, showing Gothic horseman with a prisoner: he wears splinted metal greaves on his legs, and gloves with splinted cuffs. Ninth century

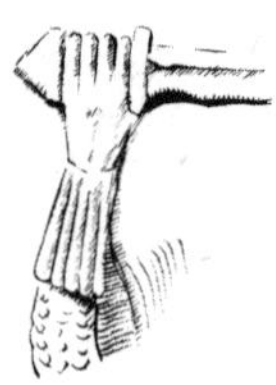

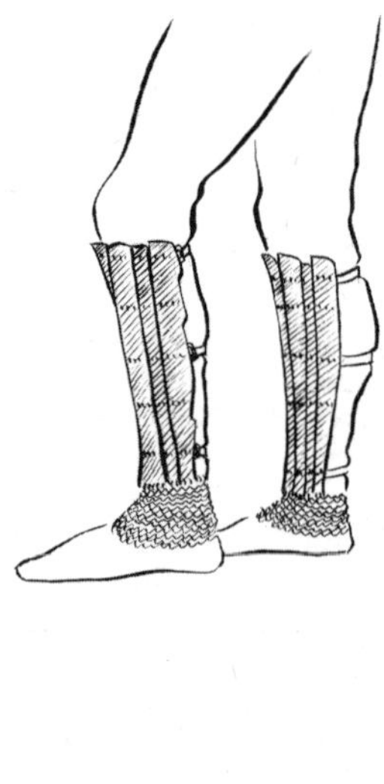

Above: splinted cuff: part of a figure from one of the plates on the Sutton Hoo helmet, seventh century

Right: pair of splinted greaves from one of the Valsgärde graves: seventh century

takes his prepared rings, and a tool like a pair of pliers; he links his ring to its neighbours, inserts a rivet into the two flattened, pierced overlapping ends of the ring and closes it in one pinch.

To the non-knitter, the process of knitting and reading knitting patterns seems a mystery and the way a garment grows under the flashing needles little short of a miracle. It was the same with mail; an experienced mail-maker could produce his shirt or hood or leggings with almost fantastic rapidity. How do I know? Well, although I have never seen it done, I know two people who have. One has actually done it, a brilliant scholar, who about fifteen years ago, by studying old mail garments, worked out the exact way in which mail used to be made. He made the tools to work with, and then proceeded to make it. The other was an old soldier who fifty and more years ago served on the North-west Frontier in India. There he once saw an old Pathan making a mail shirt. He sat at a little table outside his hut in a remote Khyber village; along the wall on the ground squatted about half-a-dozen little boys, all winding wire around rods for all they were worth. The boy at the end of the row was cutting through the wire coils and handing the rings to a man who swaged and pierced the open ends. He put the finished rings in a heap by the old man's hand and, as fast as your mother knits her jumper, the old Pathan was taking a ring and a rivet, linking the ring, putting in the rivet and closing it with his pliers.

Mail was very important to the seventh-century warrior, for it was his most usual type of body-armour. There were shirts made of tough leather—often just leather or buckskin but with hundreds of little flat plates of horn sewed to it—but such garments were much more difficult to make and far stiffer to wear; there has never been anything so hard to cut or pierce and yet so soft and flexible as mail. Its chief drawback is that it is heavy. A byrnie was usually quite short, reaching just below the hips with sleeves only to the elbow, but it would weigh nine kilos (twenty pounds) or more. This is a great weight, and seems dreadfully heavy if you hold it in your hands, but when you put it on, the weight seems almost nothing, no more than a thick overcoat. How do I know? Because I own a byrnie which I wear often when I lecture on armour, and I have worn others. This form of short mail shirt went on being used in Europe until the seventeenth century, and in the East until the present day. I should add that the one I have is not a Saxon one! It dates from about A.D. 1500, but is of exactly the same kind as an ancient byrnie. But several byrnies of the period with which we are concerned *have* been found.

You can make knitted garments which look exactly like mail; in fact you are constantly seeing them on films and television. Get someone to knit you a jersey to fit you well, using plain stitches and a No. 6 needle. You will need very fine string or macramé twine, not wool. When it's finished, dye it black. When it's dry, get some silver paint and lightly brush it over the surface. You'll be surprised how exactly like real mail it will look. You can have either a short byrnie, or a long-sleeved, nearly knee-length hauberk such as later warriors like the Normans and Crusaders used to wear.

The next item of war-gear mentioned in that passage from *Beowulf* is the shield: 'their wide, bright bucklers'. These shields were made of thin boards covered with linen and leather; one of the poetic names for a shield was 'the war-linden'.

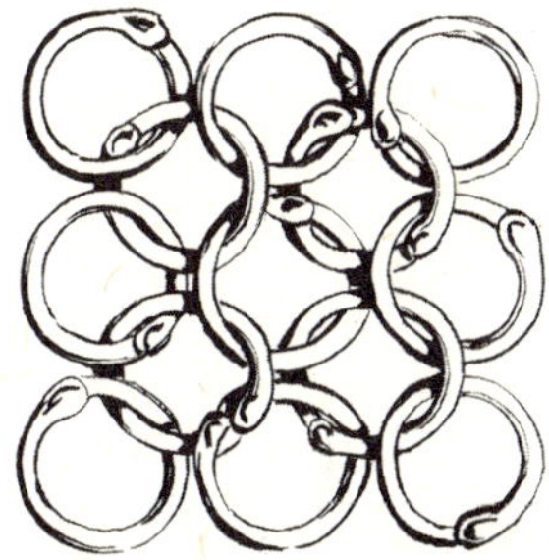

This is a section of mail. You can see why it used always to be referred to as a Net (I have described on pages 36-7 how this name originated). Each ring is linked to four others, forming an extremely strong web.

The wood was usually a close-grained wood like lime, and a round shield 70 or 90 cm (30 or 40 in.) in diameter would be made of three or four boards about 5 mm ($\frac{1}{5}$ in.) thick dowelled together edge to edge. Then both front and back surfaces were covered with glue, and a layer of linen put on. Then another coat of glue, and another linen cover, and over the front would go a facing of stout hardened leather, glued on. There was a large boss in the centre made of iron or bronze and often very elaborately decorated, and the front would be reinforced with strips of metal, iron or bronze again, and there was often a rim of metal right round the edge.

In the Sutton Hoo burial were the remains of a most magnificent shield, splendidly enriched with a gilded boss and ornaments all inlaid with garnets and coloured glass. Like all the other gear in the grave, it was in small bits when it was found, but it has been carefully put together again so that we can see it in all its original splendour. It has a rim of gilded bronze, by which it was possible to tell that its diameter was 83.82 cm (about 2 ft 9 in.) This is a very big shield, a lot broader than the ones found in the Danish bogs. It has a great iron boss ornamented with garnets and gilt bronze, and gold and gilt-bronze reinforcement in the form of stylised animals. There is a great, ferocious-looking bird of prey, a strange insect-like dragon with six pairs of legs, and a fairly simple but very elegant bar of bronze-gilt. The bronze-gilt rim was decorated at intervals with many little dragon-heads, looking very like ducks. On the left side of the shield, balancing the reinforcing bar on the right, are two large studs. These are the heads of great rivets holding the leather arm-strap to the inside of the shield.

The inside of the boss is hollow, with a stout metal bar crossing it vertically. The shield was held by putting the forearm through the leather arm-strap and holding the bar across the boss in the hand.

The leather surfaces of shields were often painted; several have been described in the sagas: in the Saga of the Volsungs, for instance, we are told of a warrior who had a splendid shield:

> '. . . of many layers, covered with red gold; and on it was painted a dragon. It was dark brown in the upper part and light red on the lower, and in the same way were coloured his helmet, saddle, and armour. He had a gold coat of mail and all his weapons were ornamented with gold and marked with a dragon, so that everyone who saw the dragon might know who this man was if he had heard that Sigurd slew the dragon called Fafnir.'

The Volsung Sigurd was, of course, the great hero whom the Germans adopted and called Siegfried.

This painting of the shield and weapons with a personal sign was a foreshadowing of the well-known later medieval idea of heraldry. Incidentally, it is interesting to hear of Sigurd's 'gold' mail shirt. It doesn't mean it was made of gold, but of gilded iron. A piece of a gilded mail coat was found in the bog-deposit at Vimose in Denmark.

The more poetic names for the shield are particularly good: 'The Sun of Battle' they called it, or 'The Board of Victory', 'The Sun of the Sea-kings', 'The Hall-roof of Odin', 'The Battle-shelterer', 'The Burgh of Swords'.

What would the 'stout spears' which 'stood in a stack together' have been like? Well, generally a spear is a spear and there's an end on't, but there were very many different kinds of spear found in the bog-deposits and the graves, and different kinds are mentioned in the sagas. Basically there are three kinds: the light throwing spear, or javelin; the stout, heavy thrusting spear; and a kind called '*hoggspjot*' in old Norse, a hewing spear. It is not really possible from the surviving archaeological examples to see what difference in shape there was between the thrusting and hewing spear; it depended how you used it. Rather than trying to describe the shape of the heads of these spears, I have drawn some found in the bog-deposits and some found in the graves. They are shown overleaf.

The shafts varied in length, between 3.35 and 1.52 metres (between about 11 ft and 5 ft), their lengths probably the personal choice of the original owner of the spear.

They had excellent poetic names, too. 'Serpent of Blood', 'The Flying Dragon of the Fight', 'The Sounding Fish of the Armour', 'The Snake of the Corpse' are a few of them.

Now we have had a look at the warrior's helmet, mail shirt, shield and spears, but we can't suppose that he went into battle with just these. What else did he wear? It is very uncomfortable to wear mail next to the skin, and it would be no joke fighting

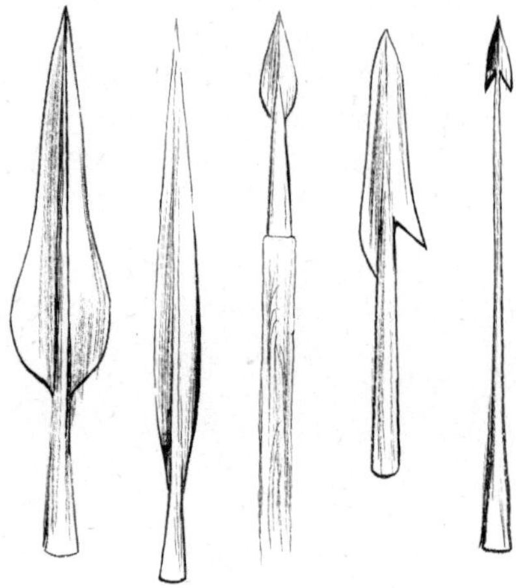

Various spear-heads, fourth to eighth centuries

barefoot. So under your mail-shirt you would need a stout tunic of wool or —preferably—hide, and under that, again, some sort of a shirt. Though mail was very resistant to the blows of sword or axe or the thrust of spears, being flexible it could not protect the body from severe bruising or broken bones; even with a stout leather jerkin under it, a man would get badly mauled, though not really injured. These Norse warriors, as well as their Celtic forebears and their Viking descendants, wore loose-fitting trousers on their legs, wrapped round between knee and ankle with thongs. The pair of trousers from the Thorsbjerg bog have socks of the same material sewn to the bottoms of the legs, but it was probably again a matter of preference if a man wore his socks this way or separately as we do now. The shoes were rather like slippers, made of leather, as far as we can tell. Several shoes or fragments of shoes have survived, and there are very many shoes shown in manuscript paintings, wall paintings and sculptures. There are a few which look like short boots; and it seems that long boots like our riding-boots were worn as well.

This was the warrior's basic clothing, worn with his armour. He'd have a cloak too, of course, but would not fight in it. In the same way he'd probably go about in a hat, and carry his helmet.

Most of these Teutonic peoples in the northern lands fought on foot; they used horses to get about, but dismounted to fight. Not so with their cousins, the Goths, Burgundians and Longobards who migrated from the north during the first and second centuries. They went into the land of the Scythians and Sarmatians, in what is now South Russia. On these vast rolling grass-lands for many centuries had lived nomadic folk who were horseman; not just the warriors, but women and children as well rode everywhere all the time. They bred very tough small ponies, like Welsh mountain ponies, or Exmoor or New Forest ponies. The Scythians who lived there from perhaps about 900 B.C. were bow-using fighters, and they fought on their ponies, moving very fast and shooting very straight from the saddle. But at some time—about 100 B.C.—they were invaded by fierce warrior tribes called Sarmatians from central Asia further to the East, who rode bigger horses and wore armour, fighting on horseback, and carrying long broadswords and long lances. They soon overcame the Scythians, and settled down on their grazing-grounds. Some two hundred years later, bands of Goths began to come, first to raid and then to settle in the same way as the Saxons and Angles began to raid and settle in Britain. These Goths

Scythian horseman

were on the whole better men than the Sarmatians, and very soon they had settled down with them—or overcome them; at this long time after we can't tell which. Whatever it was, they adopted, and improved upon, their fighting methods. When in A.D. 376 they defeated the entire East Roman army at Adrianople, and thereafter invaded and settled down in Italy and Spain and northern France, they were horse-warriors; the exact prototypes and direct ancestors of the knights of the Middle Ages.

The Burgundians and Longobards were cousins of the Goths, were in fact part of the great Gothic migrations from the shores of the Baltic to South Russia. They settled in western Europe, the Burgundians along the valleys of the Rhone and the upper Rhine, and the Longobards in northern Italy, which soon came to be called Lombardy.

We have to remember that though these peoples came from the same regions as the Swedes, Norwegians, Danes, Angles and Saxons, and though their languages remained much the same, their methods of fighting had become quite different. But the armour and weapons they fought with were just like those used in the north, and probably came from the same centres of production.

CHAPTER 3

THE SWORD: THE SERPENT OF BLOOD

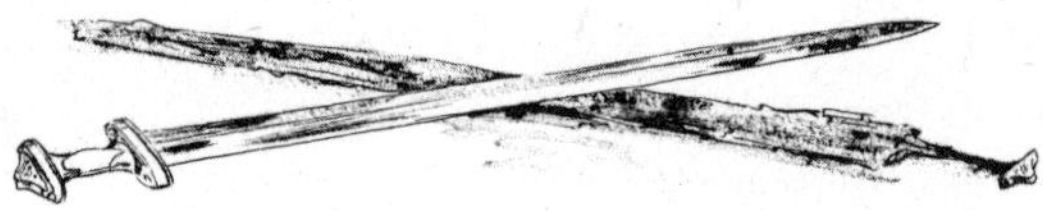

THE CENTURIES between A.D. 400 and 750 have left us a great many swords; in almost every provincial museum in the British Isles and all over the continent of Europe as well, you may find one or two, but often they look terribly disappointing; just a more-or-less flat bar of reddish brown stuff which looks like toffee, sometimes with a little piece of gold or silver sticking to it somewhere. Such swords, which have mostly been dug out of graves, bear about as much relation to the splendid and heroic weapons so greatly loved by the old warriors as a tatty, battered old car-body on a dump bears to the swift gleaming vehicle which once was someone's pride and joy. It is a great temptation to believe that swords of this remote period were always shapeless and brown or black, but of course it is not so at all. They were magnificent-looking things, their splendid gleaming blades mounted in hilts richly decorated with goldsmith's or jeweller's work.

In examining the swords of these people, we had better take them in three parts, in order of importance. First the blade, then the hilt, then the scabbard and its mountings.

These swords were neither very big nor very heavy. The average size of a blade would be 71.12 cm long by 5.08 cm broad (about $2\frac{1}{4}$ ft by 2.3 in.), and it would weigh about .68 kg (about $1\frac{1}{2}$ lb.). All of them were flat, with a wide shallow groove called a 'fuller' running the whole length from the hilt to the point. This was a means of lightening, yet at the same time stiffening, the blade; you will often hear it called a 'blood-channel', but this is nonsense; romantic-sounding, a bit gruesome, yes, but nonsense all the same. I shall be telling you some of the technical names these Germanic folk had for parts of these swords later on; they are very much more romantic, and lots more gruesome, than the old blood-channel stuff.

A sword was put together in a very simple way; the diagram will show you more clearly than a description how it was done.

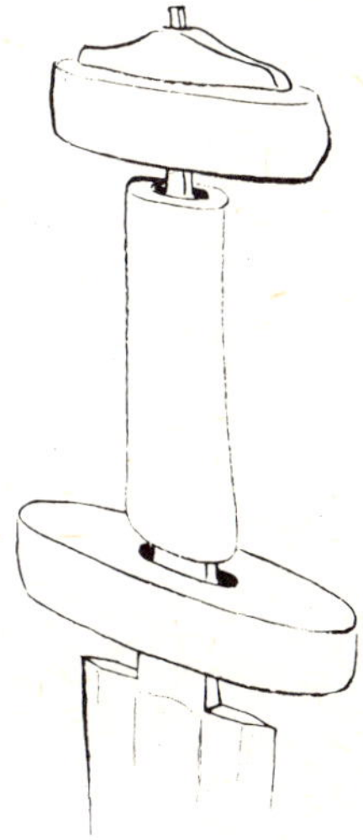

The assembly of a sword-hilt

The blade of a sword is made with a narrow extension at the end furthest from the point. This is called the Tang. It was not 'fire-hardened' like the rest of the blade but was often welded into the blade as the handle is spliced into a cricket bat. Each part of the hilt—lower guard, grip, upper guard and pommel—was pierced with a hole to fit the tang; they were fitted over it in the correct order, and the end of the tang which protruded from the top of the pommel was hammered over, forming a rivet which set the lower guard firmly against the 'shoulders' of the blade, and held all the other parts tight.

As you can see, the blade is the essential basis of any sword, and is itself an integral and vital part of the handle.

Swords of this kind had been made in Europe by the Celtic peoples of Gaul for many centuries before the time of our Saxons and Geats and Scyldings. There was little difference in the shape of a blade made, say, in what is now Austria in 300 B.C. from one made on the upper Rhine in A.D. 500; both were made of iron, hardened in various ways by the exposure of the hot metal to carbon during the forging. The result was a steely, or carburised, iron; not steel as we know it, and it was not particularly hard. It was possible to get a good edge on it, but it tended to get blunt fairly quickly and even the best blades showed a frightening tendency to bend during a fight; we often read of warriors having to straighten out their swords under their feet in the middle of a battle.

There is evidence in the poems and sagas that the sword-smiths (who we must remember were regarded as super-beings endowed with magical powers) tried all sorts of ways to make their blades harder; by quenching the glowing iron in honey or oil, or the urine of a goat or a red-haired boy, or the water of a particular stream, or, in one recipe, a mixture of the juice of radishes mixed with chopped earthworms! We can read how the smith Velent (another, Norse, name, for the more familiar Saxon, Weland) once made a sword, but wasn't satisfied with it, so he got a file and filed it all away. Then he collected the mass of iron filings and, little by little, mixed with meal, fed them to his fowls. He gathered up their droppings and burnt them, thus regaining his filings. When all the filings had passed through the chickens, he melted them down into an ingot, and forged his blade again. This he did twice more, but in the end he had a blade with which he could feel satisfied.

There are many other such stories of blade-making, all of them perhaps seeming very fanciful, but in fact they are all technically sound and would very probably achieve the desired result. Certainly the fowl-dropping idea is scientifically a good one, for the exposure of the iron to the chemical processes in the birds' bowels would tend to purify it by separating the slag.

However, at some time around the beginning of the Christian era, somebody, somewhere (and so far we have no idea who, or where) hit on a much more reliable method of hardening iron blades. The process was complicated, but not so tedious as Velent's chicken-feed method. A core to the blade was made by forging rods of good carburised iron, twisting them, laying groups of two or four of them side by side and welding them together. This process ensured that the carburised parts of the iron—the outside surfaces of the twisted rods—were carried right through the whole of this core. Then separate strips for the edges, again made of carburised iron, were welded to each side of the core. This produced a fairly thick bar a few inches longer than the finished blade needed to be. It was, of course, just a bar, and it had to be filed and ground down to the desired thickness. When this part of the forging was done, the smith had a tough, yet very flexible blade. Now he burnished it and, finally, etched it—that is, he treated the surface with some sort of acid, such as sour beer, or tannic acid, or he may have used urine or vinegar. Whatever was used, the result was that when the core part of the blade had been filed* into shape, a pattern like the markings on a snake's back showed up in the broad shallow fuller. This was caused by the twisted rods which

*One of the poetic names for a sword was 'Survivor of the Files'.

made up the core, for the more carburised parts would show up lighter than the soft iron.

Many varieties of pattern-welding were produced according to the way in which the rods were grouped and twisted. Some—most of the earliest ones—show a simple herring-bone pattern, but many have all sorts of patterns, often three or four different kinds in one blade. I have drawn some of these patterns so as to give you an idea of the kind of thing that was done.

The makers and owners of these blades regarded them as almost priceless treasures, as indeed they were, for as well as being splendid weapons, tough yet light and flexible with edges which could be ground to razor-sharpness, they looked beautiful. The etching process slightly coloured the surfaces,

Pattern-welding: (a) 'Ann' pattern (b) 'Blodida' pattern

different tints of brown or pale yellow or blue being produced by different acids, and the play of light upon the clearly marked patterns must have been fascinating to look at.

Let's see what Cassiodorus, secretary to Theodoric the Ostrogoth, Emperor of Rome, wrote about blades like this some fifteen hundred years ago. A Germanic tribal chief, a king of the Warni, had sent rich gifts to Theodoric, and Cassiodorus, writing in Latin, sent a letter of thanks from the Emperor:

'Together with musical instruments of pitch-black wood and boys with the fair skin of their race, Your Fraternity has chosen for us swords capable even of cutting through armour, which I prize more for their iron than for the gold upon them. So respendent is their polished clarity that they reflect with faithful distinctness the faces of those who look upon them. So evenly do their edges run down to a point that they might be thought not shaped by files but moulded by the furnace. The central part of their blades, cunningly hollowed out, appears to be grained with tiny snakes, and here such varied shadows play that you would believe the shining metal to be interwoven with many colours. This metal is ground down by your grindstone and vigorously burnished by your shining dust until its steely light becomes a mirror for men; this dust is granted you by the natural bounty of your land, so that its possession may bestow singular renown upon you. Such swords by their beauty might be deemed the work of Vulcan, who is said to have perfected his craft with such art that what was formed by his hands was believed to have been wrought by power not mortal but divine.'

Where Cassiodorus the Roman wrote 'Vulcan', of course the German would understand 'Weland'.

Here we have not only the blades' appearance described, but a good deal of information about some of the processes of making them. But what's this 'shining dust'? '*Splendidissimus pulvis*', Cassiodorus says, and if we knew exactly where the Warni came from, we would be able to say with certainty what it was, and where these fine blades were made. We do know more or less the regions which this small tribe inhabited round about A.D. 500, and the 'shining dust' is obviously something which is of great value in the manufacture of fine blades. However, we have two clues which give us a good deal to go on. Several years later, in 507, Cassiodorus wrote again to the King of the Warni asking him to join an alliance against Clovis, King of the Franks, and it seems that at that time the Warni inhabited the land on the lower reaches of the River Elbe; later still they seem to have been higher up the river to the south-west of Berlin. That's our first clue. The second is that in precisely these regions an abrasive polishing compound known as *Kieselguhr* is found; and it could well be *splendidissimus pulvis*. Putting these two things together, it does seem as if these wonderful blades were made in that region.

Today it is not possible to see any of these swords in all their original beauty. Many have survived, certainly; some, where the corrosion of the blade has eaten away the softer parts of the iron, show up the patterns very clearly; but others, where a hard black coating or patina—formed by the chemical action of the mud in which the sword has lain—has covered the whole surface of the blade, do not show the patterns at all. Still others were buried in their scabbards; blade and scabbard have corroded together, forming a solid and inseparable mass of rust. In these cases it has been possible by taking X-ray photographs to see the patterns. But this only shows the pattern that was there; it shows none of the beauty. You would never believe '. . . the shining metal to be interwoven with many colours'.

There is one sword, though, which you can see in pristine condition. It was made only a few years ago when the processes of making pattern-welded blades were being carefully and painstakingly worked out; it is today in the Science Museum in London. And I hope that one day a well-preserved pattern-welded blade, which hangs on my wall, will have all its black patination carefully removed by electrolysis, after which it will be cleaned, burnished and etched in the ancient manner, and again we shall be able to see what Cassiodorus saw.

A considerable number of blades of this period have been very thoroughly analysed. Many have been X-rayed, and a few have been carefully cut into sections so that the inside of the blades could be examined microscopically, and bits of them have been broken down to show the crystalline and molecular structure of the iron. It is from the basis of such analytical studies that the methods of making pattern-welded blades have been worked out and reproduced.

Not all blades, of course, were pattern-welded. A lot of them were of simple construction with more, or less, carbon in the iron; often this has been found to have been very irregularly distributed along the blade, so that it had very tough patches and rather soft ones. Such a blade would bend easily. In one of the later sagas we read of a warrior named Steinthor, an Icelander, who had a blade like this. His hilt was of splendid workmanship, all inlaid with silver, but in a fight at Swanfirth '. . . he found that the beautifully wrought sword wouldn't bite when it hit armour, and he often had to stop and straighten it under his foot'.

The manufacture of these pattern-welded blades continued until about the middle of the eighth century, but by that time the smiths had found still better ways of making even harder and better blades of steel, and there was no longer any need for the complexity of pattern-welding. Even so, many of these old blades continued in use and were regarded as great treasures and rich heirlooms for many centuries. In Zurich there is a sword of a type called a 'Landsknecht sword', very popular among the Swiss and German mercenary armies of the late fifteenth and early sixteenth centuries; mounted in its early-sixteenth-century hilt is a fine pattern-welded blade which must have been made a thousand years earlier!

So much was it the custom to hand on fine blades generation after generation that in Anglo-Saxon poetry, even in prosaic things like Wills, the term 'ancient heirloom' was often used as a synonym for a sword.

At a somewhat later period, when pattern-welded blades were still in use, we find that a general term for such a blade was 'Wave-sword' (*Vaegir* in Old Norse, *Waegsweord* in Anglo-Saxon) and we sometimes read—in *Beowulf* for example—of a sword 'patterned with venomous twigs'; but men also referred to the patterns specifically. The herring-bone pattern they called *Ann*, an Old Norse word meaning swathes of mown corn. The pattern looking like ripples on water they called *Blodida*, or 'Blood-eddy'. Even better is the name for the pattern made up of long parallel stripes down the length of the fuller ; *Idvarp*, they called it. Now *Idr* here means intestines, or guts. *Varp* is the weaving-word 'warp'. Very imaginative: your long striped pattern is the warp; the weft is the innards of your opponent, and when the warp of your sword goes through his weft, you have your completed web! They used *Blodvarp* too for this pattern.

Of course, as with armour and spears, they had many grand expressions for swords: 'Odin's Flame', 'The Ice of Battle', 'Serpent of the Wound', 'Dog of the Helmet', 'Battle-snake', 'Battle-fire', 'Fire of Shields', 'Torch of the Blood', 'Snake of the Byrnie', 'The Sea-King's Fire', 'Tongue of the Scabbard', 'The Byrnie's Fear', 'Harmer of War-knittings', and 'Widow-maker'.

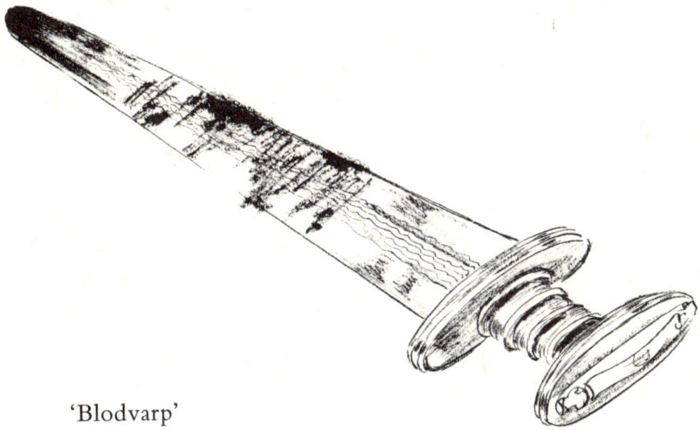

'Blodvarp'

The blades of swords are fairly easy to describe, for they were all more or less alike. They were straight and two-edged, with a fuller down the middle running the whole length. Whatever variations they showed were slight. A few, for instance, had a double fuller—two parallel grooves—instead of one. Their size varied somewhat, of course, because the men who used them were of different sizes too. But that's about all, except for the different patterns of pattern-welded blades. Not so with their hilts. These show almost infinite variety, within certain limits, but they do also show a distinct progression from the forms of the second century A.D. to those of the eighth. It is also possible to tell to some extent where they came from or were used. However, we must remember two very important things. Blades were generally made in a few centres of production, and exported all over Europe, whereas the hilts they were mounted in were made locally. So it is only by hilt-forms that we can say a sword is of Swedish, or Frankish, or English origin. Many typically English or Frankish hilts have been found in Scandinavia, and Swedish or Danish ones in England or France.

If blades were exported from a few centres, completed swords moved around to a tremendous extent. They passed from hand to hand as gifts, or trophies of battle; and the warriors who used them travelled widely with them. So a sword found in Spain may well be of Danish design because its Danish owner (a) lost his sword in Spain; (b) gave it to a Spanish warrior; (c) had it taken from him by one; (d) died in Spain and had his sword buried with him; or (e) was defeated in a battle and had his sword put on a ceremonial pile. We can very rarely say. The only guide we have in saying that such-and-such a hilt type is English or Danish or Swedish is that more of that particular type have been found in England or Denmark or Sweden than anywhere else.

We can tell the date—roughly—of these hilt types either because of the date of the graves they were found in, or by their appearance in the Danish bogs. The four main deposits, Thorsbjerg, Vimose, Nydam, and Kragehul cover the whole period from about A.D. 150 to A.D. 500; types found in the earlier deposits don't appear in the later ones, and vice versa.

There are four main types of hilt which were in use during the Migration Period; each main type had many variations and sub-types, but we cannot go into detail here. The drawing on page 60 shows the four basic types; No. 1 type has been found with associations dating it as early as about A.D. 150, No. 4 in the same way dating its latest appearances about A.D. 700. Within the five-and-a-half centuries between A.D. 150 and 700 there was, of course, a good deal of overlapping; we find examples of Type 1, for instance, in dateable finds two

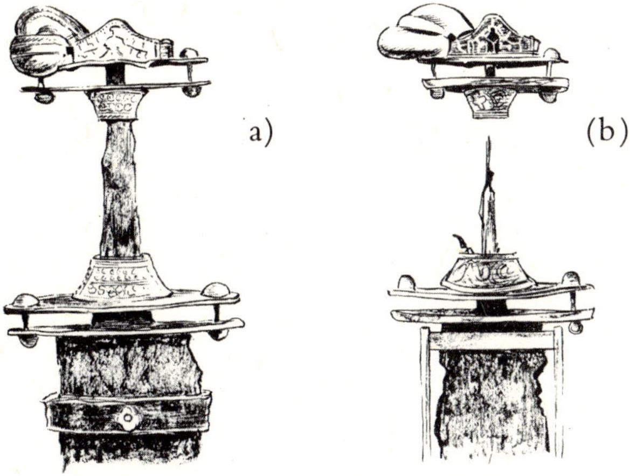

Ring-swords: (a) from Sweden (b) from Italy

or more centuries after its earliest appearance; swords were often in use for many generations.

Some modern writers, when describing a sword, speak of it as if it is seen point upward, but this does not correspond with ancient practice, so we will talk about them as we always see them in drawings or photographs or displayed in museums, with the hilts up and the point down. This is how the old Norse people described them, too.

A sword-hilt of this period has four parts: on top, the pommel; below that, the upper guard; then the grip, then the lower guard.

Until quite recently (some hundred and fifty years ago) the grip was always called 'the handle', and in describing knightly swords of the Middle Ages, we speak of the lower guard as the cross, and the upper guard disappears, leaving only the pommel. But as we are discussing swords of the Migration Period

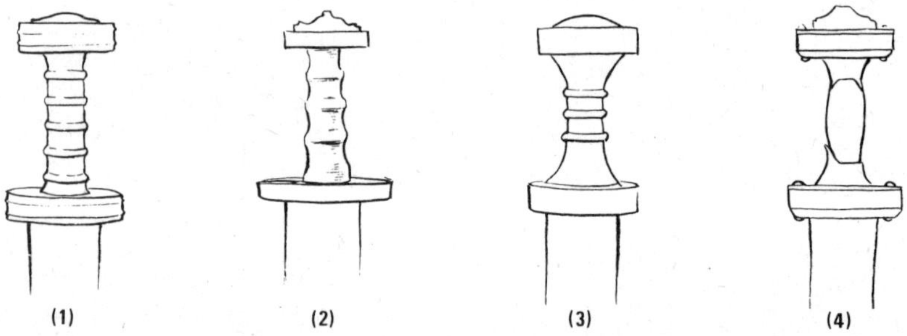

The four basic types of hilt

between the Roman Period and the Age of the Vikings, we must stick to the terms they used then.

Type I is a simple hilt with a short, stout lower guard, a grip indented by ridges to give a secure hold to the fingers, an upper guard of the same shape as, but a bit shorter than, the lower guard, and a very small, flattish pommel on top to hold the rivet of the tang. (Look back at the drawing showing how the hilt is put together.) Most of the hilts of this kind which have been found are made of wood, or horn, or walrus tusk, but some were plated with silver or bronze—and probably gold, though so far no gold-plated one has been found. There was a particularly fine silver-plated one in the Thorsbjerg deposit. This is shown on the facing page.

There is good evidence of this type being used over a span of five centuries. The Thorsbjerg one dates at, say, A.D. 200, but two more were found at Kragehul, and nothing in that find is earlier than 400. Yet another was found in a grave at Evebo in Norway which dates from about A.D. 580. That's a period of three hundred and eighty years for the same hilt-form to be in use.

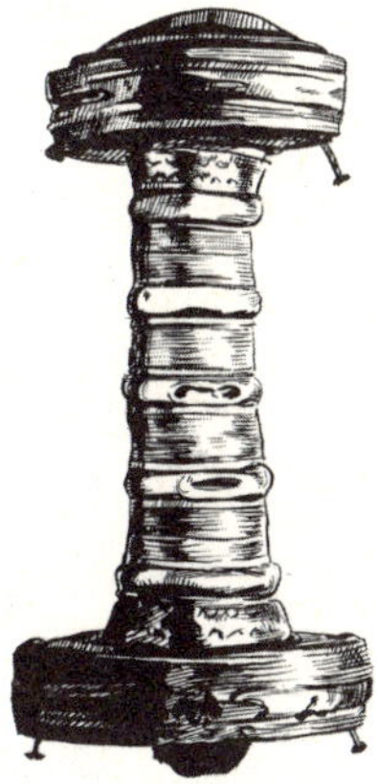

Shown on the right is a hilt from the Thorsbjerg bog-deposit. This is of wood overlaid with silver. The thick overlay of silver has preserved the wood beneath it, which in its turn has held the shape of the silver, preventing its being crushed and distorted by the pressure of the peat around it. The iron of the blade, though, has completely rusted away. This is a fine example of the Type 1 hilt shown in the diagram on the facing page. It dates from about A.D. 200.

What we *cannot* tell is whether, say, a Kragehul sword was a new one when it was put in the deposit or whether it had been in use for two hundred years already. Probably the latter. Most hilts of this type have been found in Denmark, Norway and England.

A prototype of Type 2 is one of the best-known swords of our period; it was found in the seventeenth century in the grave of the Frankish king, Childeric I, and in 1665 was presented to Louis XIV. It was found with several other things and a sax—a short one-edged sword about which I shall write presently. The hilt is jewelled with inset garnets in the same manner as is the sword from our own Sutton Hoo ship-burial. Childeric I died in A.D. 431, so the sword dates before that. A similar one in remarkably good condition was found at Klein Hunigen in Switzerland; it has all its fittings complete, but its upper and lower guards have disappeared, probably because they were made of something like ivory, which has perished in the soil in which it was buried. One is reminded of a piece from

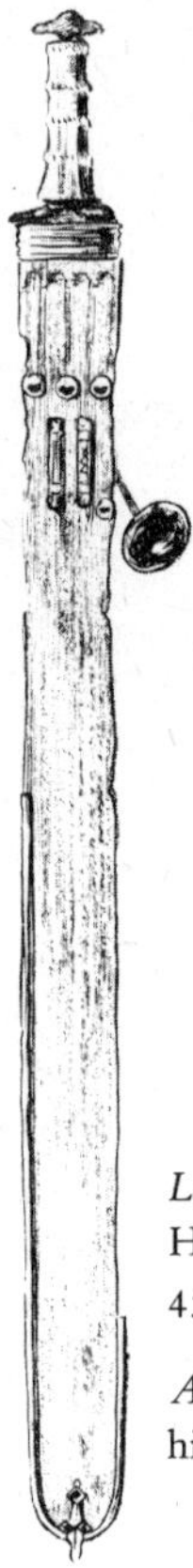

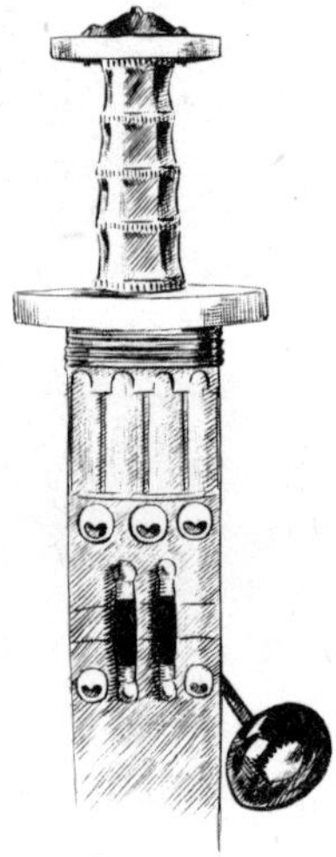

Left: Sword from Klein Hunigen, Switzerland, *c.* A.D. 450

Above: The Klein Hunigen hilt reconstructed

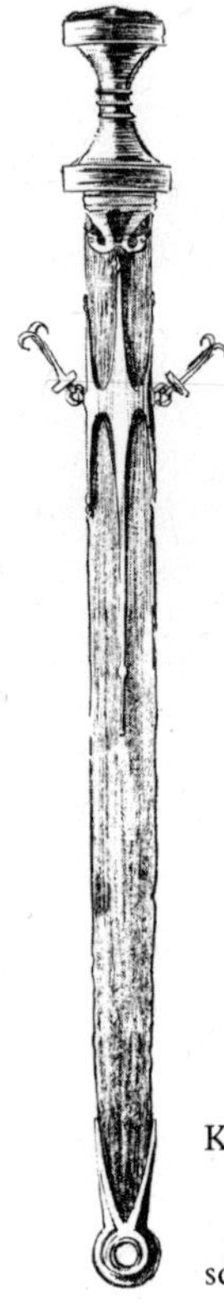

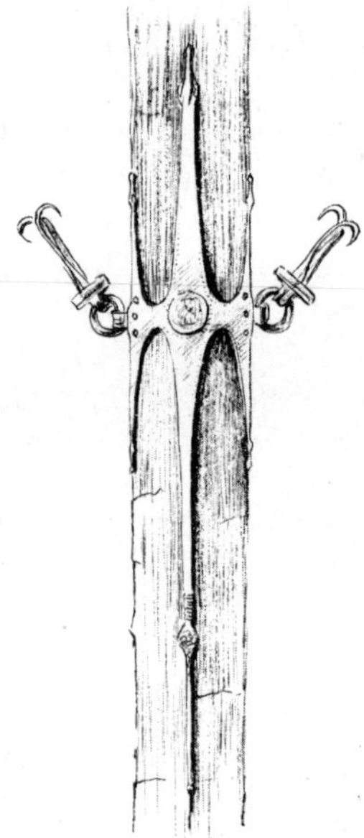

Left: sword from the Kragehul bog, *c.* A.D. 500

Above: enlargement of scabbard-mounts

the Saga of Magnus Barefoot which might refer to just such a weapon: 'He was girt with a sword called Legbiter; its guards were of walrus tusk, and its hilt (grip) was covered with gold. It was the best of weapons.'

The distribution of finds of Type 2 hilts suggests that they were in use mostly in central and eastern Europe, but Type 3 seems to have been almost exclusively Danish. It is an odd, rather clumsy-looking shape, but remarkably comfortable to hold, as I know from experience of handling one.

Two of the best examples are from the Kragehul bog, though there were some at Nydam and Vimose. The two in question, like the Klein Hunigen sword, retain their scabbards and mounts which I will describe later, but their blades show a very interesting thing; they are of about the same length, and have the same kind of hilt and scabbard-mounts. But the blade of one is broad, with edges running nearly parallel to a rounded point, while the other is narrower and tapers to a sharp point. Now in the poems there are two words, both applied to swords, which suggest that they mean different kinds of two-edged sword. The words are *Svaerd* and *Maekir*. *Svaerd* is common enough for we still use it as our own word 'sword', and it seems to have referred to the ordinary broad-bladed slashing sword. But *Maekir* is not so common; the context in which it is used suggests a sharply-pointed weapon. In these two Kragehul swords we have examples of the different blades.

Swords of Type 4 are found all over Europe and date between about A.D. 500 and 700. Nearly every sword of this period is of this type, and it had many variants; it includes the swords found in most of the Anglo-Saxon graves in England. Its principal feature is that the pommel now becomes much more important; in the previous type it had only been an elongated metal block to give a firm backing to the clinching of the tang-rivet. Here it is of a recognizable cocked-hat form set on top of the upper guard. Now the tang doesn't go right through the pommel, but is clinched over on top of the upper guard. The pommel is secured to this by long rivets which go right through each end of the upper guard. These hilts of Type 4 were more complex in make than the earlier ones, for the upper and lower guards were generally made each of three parts. The wood or ivory or horn bar was sandwiched between two metal plates, cut to the same shape as the bar itself, the lower one generally being thicker. The whole of this sandwich, filling and metal, was held together by a long rivet at either end. The knobbed heads of these rivets became an integral part of the hilt; and the rivets of the upper guard assembly held the pommel on. I have drawn a splendid sword from a Saxon grave at Coombe in Kent to show how such a hilt was made. The sword (it is in the museum at Saffron Walden in Essex) is now in fragments, but I have drawn it as it was in the days of its original splendour with its metal-work of gilded bronze.

Many of these hilts were of gold or silver, others of gilded or plain bronze, and many and various were the kinds of decoration. Perhaps the most common was the use of finely cut garnets let into 'cloisons'—little cells like in a honeycomb—of gold. This technique was practised all over Europe, and singularly beautiful it was. The plain cocked-hat-shaped pommel of the Sutton Hoo sword was like this.

One feature which we find on a few of these Type 4 hilts is the addition of a ring to one side of the pommel. For a long time it was thought that such rings were connected with the use of what were called 'Fridbond', peace-strings. These were some kind of attachment by which the sword could be tied into its scabbard so that it could not be drawn hastily. There are many references in literature to these peace-strings, but archaeologically no trace of any has ever been found; however archaeologists believed that the rings were there for the purpose of fastening the peace-strings to them. But only very few swords had rings. And many of the rings were in fact dummy ones, mere knobs through which not even a thread could be passed. Then it was thought that a ring on a hilt indicated the weapon of a king or a great chief. After all, rings had great significance, and a chieftain was often called 'Giver of Rings'. Oaths were sworn on rings, and on sword-hilts too. Maybe a ring on a king's sword had a kind of symbolic extra significance in oath-taking ceremonies.

But hardly any ring-swords were found in the graves of kings, only of simple warriors; and the swords which were found in kings' graves rarely had rings. In recent years a closer examination of ringless swords has shown that some once had rings on their hilts; had them on long enough too, to wear a distinct dent in the metal of the pommels to which they were fastened, dents similar to those where the rings are still present. No, it seems that the ring was some sort of reward for valour or a badge of rank which, given by a chief, applied only to the man who earned it. The fact that so many are still in place suggests that if the sword was laid in the grave with the man who had earned the ring, it was allowed to stay. It was only removed if someone else took the sword. After all, *you* can't wear your grandfather's D.F.C.

The earlier rings, many of which were found in Kentish graves, were small open rings fastened to the pommel by being looped through a second half-ring. Very soon the ring itself became fixed to the half-ring, then it was made as a part of it, and then the whole thing was stylised into a solid knob, shaped like the ring clasped by the half-ring. I have shown on page 68 examples of how they were made and fixed.

Of all the weapons that man invented before the pistol,

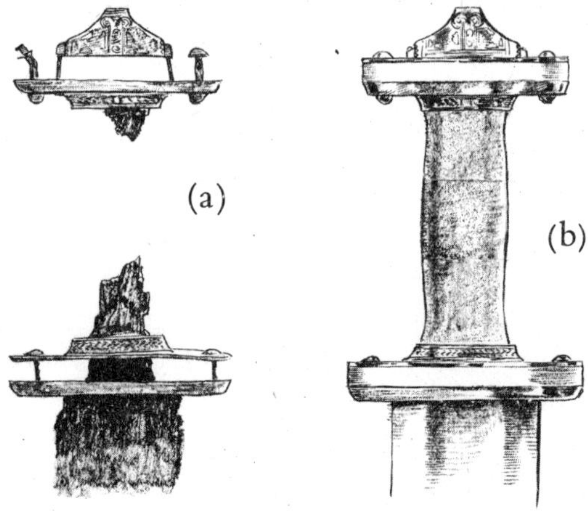

Sword from a grave at Coombe, Kent; seventh century:
(a) as it is now (b) reconstructed

Ring-sword from an Anglo-Saxon grave at Dover, Kent: seventh century

the sword was the only one (apart from its little brother, the dagger) which was always enclosed in a tightly fitting case. This was because it was always carried on its owner's person, but maybe there was a much deeper reason for it being protected so carefully. Always, from its earliest appearance in the Bronze Age, the sword has been held in great awe and respect as something symbolic of power and chieftainship; near-magical powers were attributed to it, and it was regarded as a thing of great and terrible beauty. So the scabbard, while protecting the sword's wearer and those near to him from its point and edges as he wore it at his waist, was in fact far more a protection for the blade itself.

People today are not accustomed to swords at all, but those who do take some interest in them or come into contact with them are more used to the very simple metal or leather scabbards of the eighteenth and nineteenth centuries; they are quite unaware of the delicate and elaborate craftsmanship which went into the making of a scabbard in earlier times.

There are several descriptions of scabbards in the poems and sagas, which are well supported by the plentiful evidence of surviving scabbards or parts of scabbards. Countless metal scabbard-fittings are left to us, but there are also enough of the wood and leather or linen parts too for us to know exactly how they were made. There is even one very well preserved one from the Middle Bronze Age, about 900 B.C.

From this remote time almost to our own day, the basic materials of a scabbard are very thin slats of wood, the same shape and size of the blade for which they are made, and a covering of leather, parchment, linen, velvet or any suitable material to bind them together.

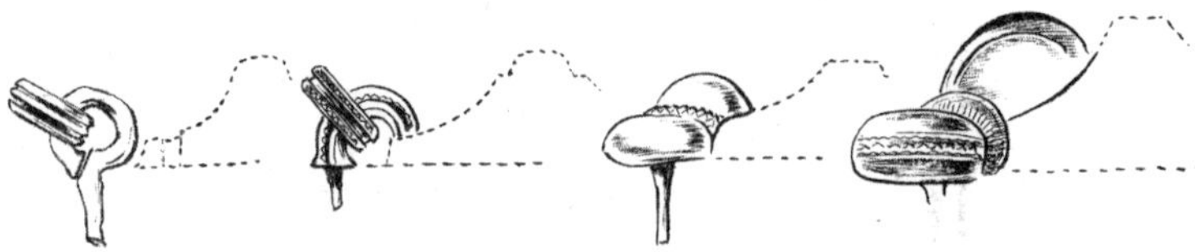

The development of the sword-ring, from *c.* A.D. 500–650

Perhaps the best example to come down to us from this period is the scabbard of the sword from the Swiss village of Klein Hunigen. This is very well preserved. It is made of two flat slats of wood a little larger than the blade. They are covered outside, and lined within, with fine leather. The scabbard is about 38 mm ($1\frac{1}{2}$ in.) longer than the blade, and in the space at the point-end there are still traces of wool; so we can tell that the point was given extra protection by a little pad of greasy natural wool. Other scabbards showing traces of wool linings have been found in Saxon graves in England. At Orsoy in France a scabbard was found lined with sheepskin, with the woolly side inwards, coming into direct contact with the blade. The fleece was fitted with the 'lay' of the wool upwards, so that the sword could be drawn out easily. In much the same way the Bronze-age scabbard I mentioned was lined with fur. This, of course was very practical, for the lanolin which is present in natural sheep's wool would protect the blade from rust. Some fragments of scabbard from English graves, looking just like odd-shaped bits of old toffee, show very clearly on their inner surfaces the impressions of fur and wool.

On some scabbards there are traces of linen covering the leather, and in a number found in Alamannic graves in Germany the covering was of birch bast.

The parts of scabbards which have survived in the greatest

quantity, of course, are the metal mounts: the mouthband, at the top of the scabbard and the chape at the bottom. In between were placed various other mounts by which the sword was fastened to the waist or shoulder-belt. These varied considerably during the five centuries with which we are concerned, and it is interesting to find that the variation was more a matter of time than of place, for the same styles of scabbard-mounts seem to have been used very widely.

Each of our four basic hilt-types seems to have had its own form of scabbard-mounts, so we must first go back again to the Type 1 hilts to examine the fittings which go with it.

The simple, functional purpose of the mouthband and chape of a scabbard is to protect the most vulnerable wood and leather parts from wear. The point-end is the part which obviously needs the most protection, and throughout the ages we find that the chape is always made to do this. During the early part of our period, from about A.D. 150–300, the chape is basically a simple 'U'-shaped metal binding for the tip of the scabbard, while the mouthband is a sort of metal collar protecting the top. There are no traces of metal fittings to fasten scabbard to belt, so presumably they were simply made of leather or cloth.

Some of the 'U'-shaped chapes had decorative designs engraved on their flat surfaces; some have been found where the bend of the 'U' has been embellished with designs cut out in the metal, while a few have the whole of the 'U' filled in with elaborate metalwork.

With the Type 2 hilts we find generally more elaborate fittings; the little cut-out metal designs in the bend of the 'U' have become definite little pieces almost of jewellery, and other metal hilt-attachments are now added. Again we must look at the Klein Hunigen sword (page 62) for its scabbard shows all the mounts used at this period (about A.D. 450). You will notice that one side of the chape has been extended until it reaches half-way up the sword's length. This is on the side of the scabbard which would tap against the wearer's leg, whether he was afoot or on horseback, and so gives strength to the edge of the scabbard where it is needed. Just below the hilt are two metal fittings sticking out, through and behind which the belt-loop can be passed, while above are three little gold discs with vaguely heart-shaped openings cut in them, with another on each side of the lower end of the strap-loops. These seem to have been simply for decoration.

With the next type, we come to the most elaborate scabbards of the whole Migration period. Mouthbands become elaborated by the addition of a pattern of stylised birds' heads cut out from the solid metal plate at the lower edge of the mouthband and the chape is now a handsome and important disc-shaped feature with stout projections springing from it to enclose the sides of the scabbard-tip. In the middle of the upper part of the scabbard we find an elaborate piece of metalwork. There is a long, flat band, tapering to each end with a slightly raised disc in the middle; attached to each side is another piece enclosing the sides of the scabbard and having a ring in its middle. To the rings are attached double hooks, like little anchors, for fastening it to—or rather, probably hooking on to—rings hanging from the belt. The whole thing is illustrated on page 62 showing one of the swords from the Kragehul bog. These hilts and scabbard-mounts date between about A.D. 400–500.

With the far more elaborate hilts of Type 4, we revert to very much simpler scabbard-mounts, a simple mouthband

and a 'U'-shaped chape, exactly the same style which we found on the Type I swords. Mind you, some of these simple fittings were extremely elaborately decorated, but with some of the very finest swords the scabbard-mounts were almost non-existent; for instance, the very rich sword from the Sutton Hoo grave had neither chape nor mouthband, only two jewelled buttons near the top on the outer side of the scabbard whose use we don't entirely understand. Some scabbards of this period, however, have survived in better condition than the Sutton Hoo one, and show in place of the metal strap-loops or studs

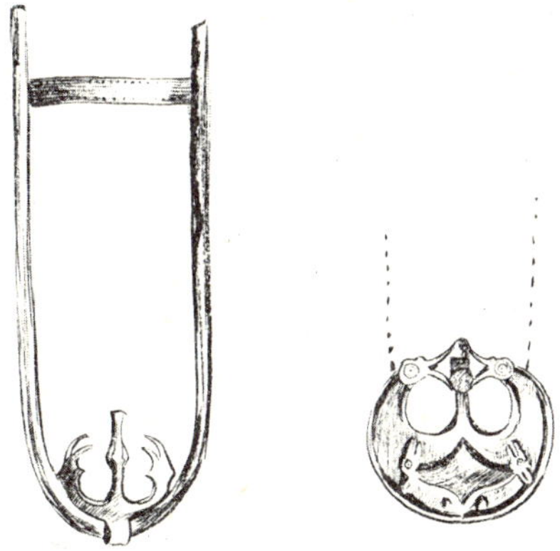

Type I scabbard-mounts

a simple wooden bar, stuck to the outer side of the scabbard with a slot between it and the scabbard to pass the belt-loop through.

If you look again at the illustration of the Klein Hunigen sword, you will see what looks like a large, dark bead sticking out from behind the scabbard. Many such beads have been found in graves, beads made of pottery or glass or crystal, in a

Jewelled ornament from the chape of the Klein Hunigen sword

few cases of meerschaum—the same yellowy-brown stuff of which meerschaum pipes are made—and, rarely, of gold and inset garnets. They are all in the shape of flattened discs with a hole through the centre, and a few have gold or silver mounts. They only appear in the graves of warriors, and only in a period between about A.D. 200 to 600. Always they are found lying close to the remains of a sword.

Now in the earlier poems we find many references to a certain kind of charm or amulet which was part of the fittings of a sword. It was called a 'Life-stone' and brought luck and victory to the sword and its owner; it had other properties too of a magical kind, for it was believed to have the power of healing any wound made by the sword to which it belonged. In the same way the knights of the Middle Ages believed that the sword which made a wound could heal it if the flat of its blade was laid on it.

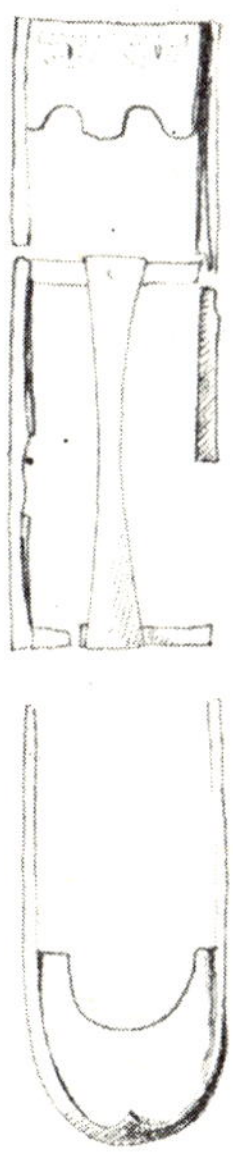

Bronze locket and chape from Sweden, *c.* A.D. 700.

Wooden scabbard bound with birch-bast, with wooden belt-loop: eighth century

There is a whole series of tales about a very famous sword called Skofnung which had a life-stone with it. It first belonged to King Hrolf Kraki of Denmark. (*Kraki* in old Norse means a pole-ladder, a stout pole with steps sticking out of either side like a telegraph pole. Hrolf was very tall and thin, hence his nickname! We would probably have called him 'Hrolf Bean-pole'.) In the saga of Hrolf's doings it simply said his sword was

(a) (b) (c)

Life-stones: (a) crystal (b) pottery (c) meerschaum, mounted with garnets set in gold (from the same grave at Morken as the helmet shown on page 36)

Skofnung, 'the best of all swords carried in the Northern lands', and that on his death it was put into his burial-mound at Roskilde with him.

We next hear of Skofnung some two hundred years later; in the saga of the early settlers in Iceland we are told that Skeggi of Midfirth, when he was passing off Roskilde in his ship, went ashore and broke into the mound of King Hrolf and took Skofnung out, along with a lot of treasure. You might suppose that after two hundred years in a grave a sword would not be much good, but these swords were very carefully greased and wrapped up before they were put in. There is plenty of evidence that weapons, swords and saxes particularly, were often taken out of graves, sometimes after only a year or two, sometimes after generations. Even a few which have survived the fifteen hundred or more years to our own day are in good shape, though a great many have perished utterly; but there is no end of difference between a spell in a royal grave of two hundred years, and one of eleven hundred or more. For one thing, the grave was not just a hole in the ground filled with earth. It was a carefully built chamber of stone or timber. The Sutton Hoo ship had a chamber amidships made of stout timber; the treasure inside it was probably dry and in perfect condition for many centuries before the timbers rotted and the chamber collapsed, letting in the damp sand which surrounded it. It is more than likely that if it had been opened in 1439 instead of 1939, everything would have been found almost as good as new.

So it would have been with Hrolf Kraki's mound. Skeggi broke into a dry, air-tight, stone chamber; he didn't dig down into damp soil. So Skofnung was bright and sharp and ready for use. It is from now on that we really hear stories about it.

Skeggi lived about the middle of the tenth century (about A.D. 950), and in Iceland at that time was a young man named Kormac, who fancied himself as a fighter, and on one occasion he borrowed Skofnung to fight a duel against a man called Bersi. Bersi was always 'going on Holmgang' (which means he was a professional duellist), so much so that folk called him 'Holmganga Bersi', much as we today might call him 'Basher Bersi'.

Kormac got tired of Bersi's boasting at one time, and said he'd fight him. But Bersi's sword, called Hviting, had a life-stone with it and Kormac's hadn't: he felt he ought to have a similar one to Bersi's to even the match. His mother told him he ought to go to Midfirth, find Skeggi and see if he could borrow Skofnung. Off went Kormac. He found Skeggi, who wasn't at all keen to lend Skofnung. He tried to put Kormac off, and said 'You and Skofnung are so different in temper; Skofnung's slow, but you are so impatient and headstrong; no, I can't lend it to you.'

Kormac went home disappointed, but his mother made him go back and try again. This time Skeggi gave in. 'All right, then; but you'll find Skofnung difficult to manage. There's a bag that covers the hilt and you mustn't disturb it; you mustn't let the sun shine on the pommel, and you mustn't draw Skofnung until you are ready to fight. You mustn't draw it when a woman is by, either. When you come to the fighting-place, go off on one side by yourself, and then draw it carefully. Hold up the blade, and blow on it, then a little snake will creep from under the hilt; slant the blade then and make it easy for the snake to creep back again.' Kormac laughed at this; and told Skeggi he must be a wizard, but Skeggi said he must do all this and it would help him in his fight.

When he got home he wanted to show Skofnung to his mother; he tried to draw it, but it wouldn't come out of the scabbard; so he tore the bag off its hilt and put his foot on the guard and tugged at the scabbard. Skofnung howled at this, but still wouldn't come.

When the time for the duel came, both Kormac and Bersi rode to the place with fifteen men apiece; Kormac got there first, and told his friend Thorgils that he wanted to sit down by himself for a minute. So he went off and unbuckled the sword and took off the bag, but he wasn't careful and the sun shone on the pommel; then he tried to draw it, but it wouldn't come until he put his foot on the guard. The little snake came out, but it wasn't handled as it should have been, and the luck of the sword was changed and it came groaning out of the scabbard.

If you had read this before reading about pattern-welded blades and seeing pictures of them, you would have thought this was awful nonsense, particularly the bit about the little snake. But if you were to have a pattern-welded sword in your hand, in pristine condition, the patterns in the middle part of the blade would seem snake-like; particularly if you breathed on them, like Skeggi told Kormac to do: your warm breath would condense on the cold iron, and as the mist passed across the blade the patterns would seem to wriggle.

Skofnung seems to have a distinct personality, and many taboos are attached to it. This was the case with most swords, but in this story we have the most complete specification of such taboos. We often read in the poems of swords coming singing out of the scabbard, or groaning or even howling. Why? This is no more fanciful than the snakes. A sword whose iron is good, and whose blade is very firmly and properly set in its hilt, rings like a bell; when you draw such a sword, even out of its soft wool lining, it will very faintly ring—or groan. (Which it does probably depends entirely upon the mood one is in when one draws the sword.) If on coming out the point, as it clears the mouth of the scabbard, very faintly taps upon the metal mouthband, it will sing (or groan, or howl) much more distinctly. I am not making this up on theory. I have a sword and scabbard like this, and it sings like anything when I draw out the sword.

Skofnung's days were not ended with Skeggi. We hear of it again early in the eleventh century when Eid, Skeggi's son, had it, though he was an old man by then. He also lent the sword, this time to a friend of his called Thorkell Eyjolfsson, who wanted to kill an outlaw named Grim who had slain Eid's son. Thorkell borrowed Skofnung and found Grim and fought him; but then he found that he liked him. He had wounded Grim in the fight, but '. . . he took Skofnung's stone and rubbed it on, and tied it on to Grim's arm, and immediately it took all the smarting pain and swelling from the wound.'

So Eid didn't get his revenge. Didn't get his sword back, either, for Thorkell kept it. Later, when Thorkell was shipwrecked off Iceland, a bit of the ship's timber with Skofnung stuck into it was washed ashore on an islet; someone found it, and recognizing it, took it to Thorkell's son Gellir. The islet was called Skofnungsey ever after.

When Gellir was old (we must be nearly up to the time of the Norman Conquest in 1066 now), he set out on a pilgrimage to Rome; but in Denmark he was taken ill, and died at Roskilde. Skofnung was never heard of again, so was probably buried with him, only a short way away from its first resting-place in Hrolf Kraki's mound.

The fact that when Skofnung was cast up by the sea it was recognized and taken to its home is an indication of the rarity of good swords, and of the fact that the weapons of heroes were just as important and interesting to ordinary folk as the heroes themselves.

The practice of naming swords, and almost every bit of personal gear as well, is about as old as time itself. The poems and sagas abound with the names of swords, saxes, spears and axes, but swords are, of course, the most important. These are personal names, not poetic expressions like 'Flame of Battle'. Some names seem to have been just names, like Odin's Gram which the Volsung hero Sigmund pulled out of the roof-tree, but others were descriptive in some way of the sword's appearance or of its qualities. Legbiter, Magnus Barefoot's sword; Quernbiter (a quern is a small grinding stone) which Olaf Trygveson had; Byrniebiter, Footbiter, Brainbiter, and so on. The hero Grettir's sword, *Aettarttangi* meaning 'Sword of Generations', is another; and perhaps the most familiar of all, the sword Hrunting which Beowulf borrowed from Unferth for his fight in the depths of the mere seems to have something to do with thrusting, its name being derived from the Old Norse verb *Hrindan*, to thrust. Several names suggest a pattern-welded blade, like King Magnus Erlingsson's Fishback.

Many sword-blades have names or marks stamped upon them, but those have nothing to do with the personal names we have been discussing nor the names of the swords' owners. They are the names and marks of the smiths who made them. (Actually, the practice of putting names and marks seems to have gone out of fashion at the very beginning of our period and did not return until after the end of it, but we must consider them to avoid confusion.)

Our period is pre-eminently the age of the pattern-welded blade, and it is only on very few of the earlier ones that we find any smiths' marks. The great majority of them had none. The marked ones belong to the late Roman period, and the names—Riccim, Tasvit, Cocillus, Ranvic—seem to be Celtic; not altogether surprising, since throughout the Roman period and for long before it the Celts were the great iron-workers. When we meet the new smith-names appearing in the ninth century, they are definitely Nordic—Ulfbehrt, Ingelri, Leutfrit, Niso, Atelbald. These names appear on the swords of Vikings, from the ninth century to the eleventh, and these are the ones you will mostly see in museums. It is just possible, though I have no evidence whatever for saying so, that the smiths who made the pattern-welded blades didn't need to use marks because each had his own distinctive and especial pattern, which would be known. Whatever the reason may be, they ceased to use marks after about A.D. 300.

Bladesmiths' marks, third and fourth centuries A.D.

These marks were made by hard stamps and dies being struck into the tang or the upper part of the blade when it was softened to welding-heat. The marks, as distinct from the names, have been found in identical form—they look almost as if they were struck by the same dies—on sword-blades dating between about A.D. 1350 and 1450, a thousand years later. The curious Y-shaped mark is inlaid with gold, which is another late-medieval practice.

Bladesmiths' names, ninth and tenth centuries A.D.

Marks of the kind shown above are of much later date than those on the facing page. The earliest of these marks cannot be before about A.D. 750, while of the others, the latest cannot date after about A.D. 400. While the former were generally stamped upon pattern-welded blades, the latter never were. And the techniques were totally different. These later, Viking Age marks were made by, first, cutting the marks with a chisel in the metal of the blade, then heating it to welding-heat together with a series of little rods of iron. The rods, forming the strokes of the letters or patterns, were then hammered into the chisel-marks, and became welded to the steel of the blade—for these blades were of steel, not carburised iron like the earlier ones. There were two kinds of mark: the names of smiths, and more-or-less geometrical patterns. A good many have been noted now; the most frequently appearing names being those illustrated here, evidence of the finds suggesting that the Ulfberht workshop began to operate earlier than the Ingelri firm, and had ceased to function before Ingelri finally ceased working, perhaps in the eleventh century. There is one curious blade (in the museum at Wisbech, Cambridgeshire) with the name INGELRI on one side and ULFBERHT on the other, though both names are badly mis-spelt. Other names of these Frankish smiths are Leutfrid (in Saxon, Leofric), Atelbald, Banto, Benno and Niso.

As well as the names, many blades had on their reverse sides patterns of obviously symbolic meaning, to which, however, we have no clues. Favourite among them was a series of upright strokes with a diagonal cross in between. Another popular one, curious to a modern eye, is a diagonal cross between two circles: OXO.

This practice of marking smith-names in inlaid iron continued into the twelfth century. Many blades have been found with the words *GICELIN ME FECIT* on one side and *IN NOMINE DOMINI* on the other, all dating between about 1100 and 1175.

These early marks, as distinct from the stamped names, are intensely interesting, for the marks stamped upon the blades of Celtic swords of A.D. 300 and earlier crop up again eleven centuries later, *the same marks*, on the blades of late thirteenth century swords and remain in use until about 1650. We cannot explain this enormous lapse of time for their disuse, but their reappearance, unchanged, after so long, indicates that the marks themselves must have been very significant. The marks of bladesmiths are closely akin to those of masons; both crafts were 'misteries' holding their origins to be semi-divine or magical. Until a lot more work has been done on these marks, they and their origins and meaning will remain, in the modern sense, a 'mystery'.

CHAPTER 4

SAX, AXE AND ARROW

I HAVE DEALT with the sword at length because it is, after all, far more important and interesting, and far more varied, than any other weapon used in this period, but we cannot ignore the axe, so much regarded as a Viking's weapon, and the different forms of sax, nor the bows and arrows which were occasionally used in war by the Teutonic peoples.

The sax probably comes next in importance to the sword; it did so in the regard of the warriors of the north, for from the Norse tales and the Scandinavian finds come the most interesting mentions of saxes and the finest surviving specimens; and it has long been a popular belief that the very name of our own ancestors, the Saxons, came from their fondness for the sax as a weapon for men.

Its use during this period ranged from that of a cooking or table knife to a weapon comparable with the long sword, and the size and shape of saxes proves this. The shape is that of a knife, but there are three distinct variations on this basic form, each variation having been used in three clearly defined regions: England; Scandinavia and North-west Germany; and the rest of Europe—except Spain and Southern Italy, where saxes don't seem to have been used at all.

The English (or Anglo-Saxon) ones range in size from a weapon as big as a sword to a knife not much bigger than a clasp-knife, but the average size of the hundreds which have been found is about 150 mm (about 6 in.) long from hilt to point. In Anglo-Saxon poetry, but particularly in Wills, a distinction is sometimes made which probably refers to these different-sized saxes, for we find the word *handseax* as well as *seax* (this, by the way, is the Anglo-Saxon spelling of the word, with an 'e' in it); *handseax* has been assumed to mean the short knife.

Many of these English seaxes are decorated with patterns or inscriptions of copper or brass or silver let into the iron of the blade; one short one in the British Museum (found at Sittingbourne in Kent) has not only elaborate patterns in silver or brass but in niello—a black composition, like black enamel—as well. It is particularly interesting because it has the name of its owner on it, and its maker too:

Biorhtelm Me Worte	*Sigeberiht Me Ah*
Biorhtelm Made Me	Sigeberiht Owns Me

These inscriptions are in Roman lettering, but another long seax from the Thames, also in the British Museum, has the entire Runic alphabet inlaid along its blade.

Incidentally, to digress for a moment: there is an unfortunate popular belief that runes are magic spells, or rhymes. They are not. They are a simple form of letters, used in northern countries and derived directly from the ancient Etruscan writing. Their virtue is that they are made up entirely from straight lines, and so can easily be cut on stone or wood or bone or iron. The Runic alphabet is called, correctly, the Futhorc, for the first of its twenty-nine letters are F, U, TH, O, R, C. So never be fooled when you read of a sword engraved with runes; it doesn't mean spells and invocations. Mind you, swords *were*

(a)

(b)

(c)

The three main types of sax-blade: (a) Anglo-Saxon (b) Frankish (c) Scandinavian

Anglo-Saxon sax, from Sittingbourne, Kent: eighth century

Anglo-Saxon sax with Runic 'Futhorc' (alphabet); from the River Thames

engraved (at a later period than ours) with spells and invocations, but they weren't runes. Even Rudyard Kipling, in one of his stories in *Puck of Pooks Hill*, called the 'The Joyous Venture', makes this mistake. The runes were the *letters*, no more.

I have drawn the Thames seax so that you can see the whole of this inlaid 'Futhorc'.

So to return to our saxes, now spelt in the Old Norse manner as we are telling about the Norse weapons. They were used, more often than swords, all through the Roman period. The earliest one which has been found in Scandinavia dates at about 300 B.C. and is of the same shape as many found in the Vimose bog six hundred years later. The hilts or handles of these are interesting, for they so closely resemble the hilts of early nineteenth-century sabres, and indeed present-day military swords. Look at the drawings on page 87 where I have drawn one sax in its scabbard from Vimose as it is now, and a reconstruction as it was when the bone or horn of its handle was still in place, and an English cavalry sabre of the 1796 pattern. You can see the similarity.

These saxes were on the average about 533.4 mm (21 in.) long from hilt to point; later, in the Viking age, the Norwegians had a fancy for even bigger saxes, hilted like swords—they *were* in fact one-edged swords although the warriors called them saxes.

The Frankish sax was generally a heavy knife, about 254 mm (10 in.) long, with a plain knife-handle on its straight tang; they, like the middle-sized English saxes, were probably very useful as weapons at close quarters, but served their more usual function about the kitchen and the farm.

Axes are difficult things to treat as weapons, for like the

Frankish sax, a domestic axe could equally well be used to fight with, or a war-axe to fell a tree. However, many splendid axes survive which are decorated in a manner which seems to make it plain that they were the tools of warriors, not of farmers.

As with so many weapons, the same shapes of axe were

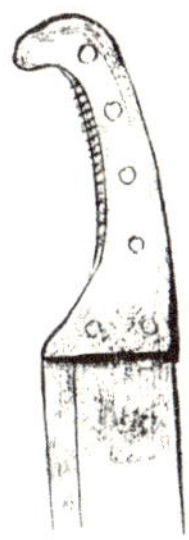

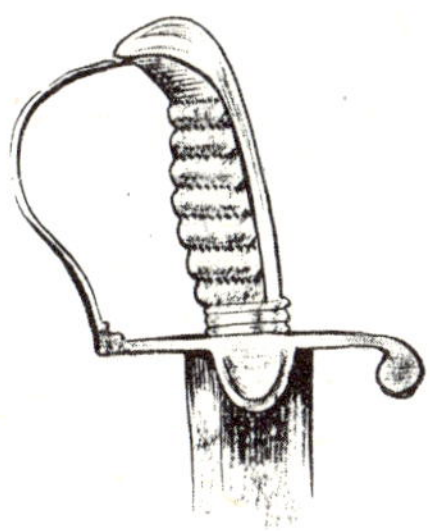

Far left: sax in its wooden scabbard, from Vimose: fifth century

Above left: sax hilt reconstructed

Above right: late eighteenth-century sabre hilt

Left: complete Frankish sax-hilt from a rich grave at Pouan in France; fifth century

used all over Europe, but there is one variation which enables us to distinguish between a Scandinavian axe-head and a Frankish one of the same shape. This is the form of the socket, the hole in the top of the axehead through which the haft goes. In the Scandinavian axes there is a sharp projection in the metal of the axe at each side of the hole whereas in the Frankish one this projection is at the top of the hole with another similar one at the bottom.

The fighting axes of these times were not so big as those used later on by the Vikings, but they were effective weapons all the same. They were about the same size as a modern felling-axe, with the same length of haft. I am speaking, of course, of the axes used by men fighting on foot; those Teutonic people who at this time fought on horseback—Longobards, Goths and some of the Franks—used rather lighter axes with shorter hafts.

There was one very specialized kind of axe in use by the

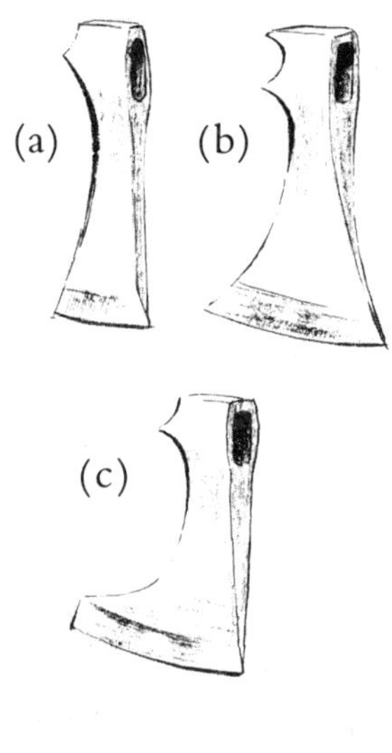

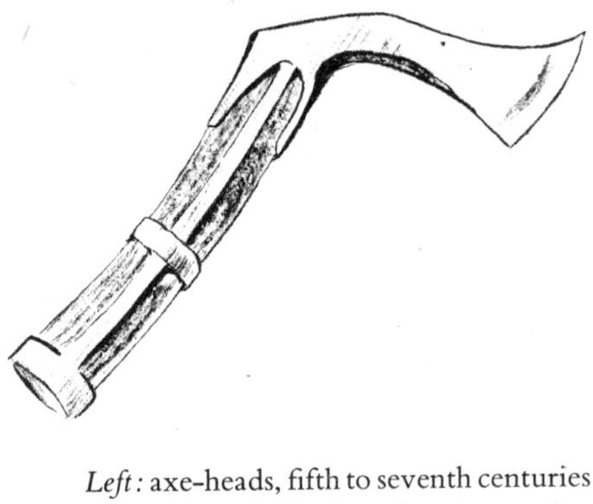

Left: axe-heads, fifth to seventh centuries A.D.; (a) and (c) Scandinavian socket (b) Frankish socket

Above: Frankish throwing-axe

Frankish tribes from perhaps the first century A.D. This was a small throwing-axe, with a peculiarly shaped head and a very short shaft. The Frankish warriors had great skill in hurling these axes, and much of their early successes against the Romanized Gauls early in the Migrations has been attributed to their skill with their national weapon. The Roman writers called the thing *Francisca* and, as with the sax and the Saxons, so it has been believed that the Franks took their name from their particular weapon. It seems rather awful that the proud name of France may owe its origin only to a nasty little battleaxe.

The Norsemen, as may be expected, had some splendid poetic expressions for an axe, often calling it 'Witch': there was 'Battle-Witch', 'Fiend of the Shield', 'Wound's Wolf', 'Witch of Helmets', and so on.

In the northern lands, the art of archery was not regarded as worthy of warriors. Bows and arrows were used in battle, of course, but the Norsemen regarded them in the same spirit as the knights of the early sixteenth century regarded the hand-gun man, as a nasty nuisance. The bow was a useful weapon for hunting, or for murder; but however they may have disliked it, there it was, and of course they made a song about it, too. In fact, some of their best expressions were given to arrows: 'The Swift-Flyer', 'Hail of Battle', 'The Glad Flyer', 'Rain of the Bow', 'War-Sleet', 'Corpse-Twigs', and so on. Many bows and hundreds of arrows have been found in the bog-burials; most of the bows were powerful weapons between 1.5 and 1.8 metres (about 5 to 6 ft) long, while arrows were between 61 cm and 91.5 cm (about 2 to 3 ft) long. They had four flights bound in with tarred twine; they were often decorated with gold, and some bore Runic inscriptions or their owners' names. The heads (or piles, as arrowheads are correctly called) were generally long and narrow, some having barbs and some not. In their shapes there is little to distinguish them from the arrows of ancient peoples such as the Greeks or Egyptians, or more modern ones such as the nations of medieval Europe.

CHAPTER 5

THE WARRIOR

THE WARRIOR who fought with the weapons we have been looking at needed to have the same kind of skill as a professional wrestler has today—instant reactions, extraordinary agility and suppleness of body, and great muscular power and control; above all, the ability to control and direct his strength. Before we discuss fighting methods, listen to this description of a fight from one of the later sagas. You remember the Icelander Steinthor of Midfirth, who had a sword with a beautiful silver-inlaid hilt but a poor blade? Well, here he is again in a very tricky fight on a little rocky islet in the middle of a frozen-over river:

'Thorlief Kimbi remarked when he saw Steinthor draw his sword, "So you are still using the silver hilt, Steinthor? But I can't tell whether you're using the same soft blade you had in Apta Firth last autumn." "I am in hopes," replied Steinthor, "that you'll have found out whether I have a soft blade or not before we part!"

And when they had been contending against each other for a good while, Thord Hawkeye made a run at the skerry and hurled a spear at Thorlief Kimbi; for he was ever in the forefront of the battle. The missile struck Thorlief's shield, and Thord was so busy defending himself that he lost his footing on the sheet of ice and fell on his back, and slid backwards off the skerry. Thorlief Kimbi sprang after him, and was going to slay him before he got on to his feet again, but Steinthor ran up and defended Thord with his shield, and with his other hand he hewed at Thorlief Kimbi and cut off his leg above the knee. At the same time another man cut at Steinthor's middle, and as he saw this he leapt into the air and the blade came between his legs; performing all three actions at one and the same instant.'

This describes things which went on in the tenth century, three hundred years after our particular period, but this sort of fighting was still going on a thousand years later, for the Scots fought with broadsword and targe up to the time of Culloden in 1746, and in Africa many of the Hausa tribes, and particularly the Hadendoa of the eastern Sudan (the famous 'Fuzzy-Wuzzies') fought with long straight swords, spears, shields and mail shirts until after 1900. What is more, in 1884 at the battle of Tamai in the Sudan they broke a British infantry square with these weapons.

You had to think quickly in this sort of fighting, and move as fast as you thought. You had to be so sharp-eyed that when your opponent threw his spear at you, you could catch it in flight, turn it and throw it back—and your throw had to be strong enough to go through him. At close quarters you used the spear as a soldier uses a bayoneted rifle; modern bayonet drill has most of the movements of spear fighting. When your man thrust at you, you had to be quick and agile enough to jump away, or jump right over the darting blade. Or you could try to catch his point in your shield and drag it out of his hand.

The Franks had a particular kind of javelin especially designed to do just the opposite, to drag the shield out of their enemies' hands. It was called an Angon, and our own Saxon ancestors in England used it too, though it never seems to have been popular in the North. It had a small barbed head set in a very long, thin, iron neck, with a hollow socket at the end of it to fit over the wooden shaft. When throwing it, the Frank aimed it at his opponent's shield. It stuck in, and the soft iron neck bent, so that the heavy shaft dragged the shield down and the warrior couldn't cover himself properly with it; he couldn't cut the spear-shaft off with his sword or axe, either, because of the long iron neck (with an ordinary javelin, it was easy enough to hack through the shaft just below the head as the spear stuck in, and free your shield).

The Franks were the most barbarous and ill-equipped of all the Migrating peoples, but they were ferocious fighters, all the same. Only the leaders wore mail, or iron helmets; the ordinary fighting man, according to many of the Roman historians, was a scruffy individual with his long, tousled hair and beard, ragged tunic and trousers, and his spear and shield and little axe. One of these historians (Agathius, writing early in the fifth century) says of them:

> 'They are a tall race, clad in close-fitting garments with a belt round the waist; they hurl their axes and cast their spears with great force, never missing their aim. They manage their shields with great skill, rushing on their enemy so fast that they seem to fly faster than their javelins.'

It must have been a terrifying experience to stand up to a charge of these people; you can just imagine them coming at you, yelling like maniacs, and the hiss and thud of those terrible little throwing axes; imagine what it was like when an Angon stuck in your shield, pulling it away from you—then the Frank would be on you, putting his foot on the bent-down spear shaft, dragging down your shield and hacking at you over the top.

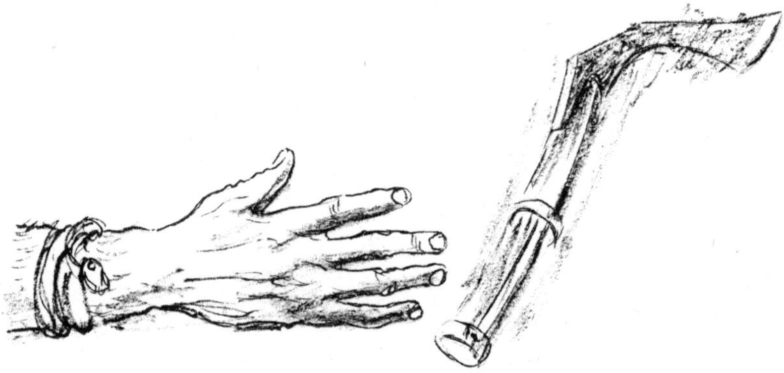

Throwing the axe

They possessed one of those qualities which almost always assures a fighter of victory—a complete disregard of their own danger, not caring a damn for their life or limb.

The Franks didn't become horsemen until after A.D. 700, outside our period, but their cousins and foes the Goths and Longobards always fought mounted. Their fighting methods were exactly the same as those of the medieval knight, with which we are familiar; but the Romans were appalled by the power of their massed charge, and the terrible effects of their long lances; they had never seen anything like it before, and it horrified them. Procopius, who was Secretary to the great Roman general Belisarius in the middle of the sixth century, wrote a History of the events of his day; it's pretty dull, but even after all these hundreds of years we can share his twinge of horror when he saw a Gothic horseman's lance go right through a Roman cavalryman. His prose for a moment glows with life as he describes how the Goth slowly raised his dripping lance, with the armoured Roman kicking and vomiting on the end of it. This feat needed not only tremendous muscles, but a tremendously tough spear-shaft.

When you fight on horseback your horse is a weapon with his teeth and hooves, but your feet and your shield are not; but when you fight on foot, your shield can be very deadly to your foe as well as a protection to yourself. If you lunge forward or downward with its rim you can knock your man off-balance, or stave in his ribs, or smash the bones of his face. With your feet, too, you can trip him, stamp on him, or kick him where it will double him up and give your sword a chance to finish him.

The blows of sword or axe had to be given with as much power and speed as you could put into them, but there was more to it than that; you had to be able to change the direction of your blow while it was still falling, to follow the movements of your opponent as he dodged or jumped away from it. And your blow had to be accurately aimed, and timed to a split second.

What about the effects of all this swift and accurate sword-play? We read a lot about heads and arms and legs being lopped off. Is it true? Well, there is plenty of evidence that it is. Evidence is not proof, but there is so much from all our three sources—the poems and sagas, the Roman historians, and archaeological finds—that the case *is* almost proved. We have another source of reliable evidence too: living eye-witnesses, with their very clear and reliable reports of sword-strokes made in blade-testing and sword fighting from Japan.

The poems and sagas, of course, abound with tales of warriors being cut down in half, and so on. Rather a more reliable account

comes from a Latin historian, Thales of Antioch, writing of how Theodoric the Great slew Odovacar, king of the Ostrogoths, in A.D. 493. This was murder, not a fight, but it was done with a sword-stroke. Odovacar had to be killed, but Theodoric's guards hesitated to slay him; so Theodoric drew his own sword and struck.

'He leapt upon him and dealt him a blow with his sword upon the collarbone. It was a killing blow; the weapon cut Odovacar's body down to the hip. It is said that Theodoric exclaimed, "God, the fellow has no bones!" '

Diagonally down from collarbone to hip! Some blow; but in old Japan a similar stroke, delivered upward, was one of the recognized strokes any respectable Samurai had to be able to make, cleanly. It was called *Iai*; its purpose was to kill your man in one blow as you drew your sword: you drew it from your left hip, and continued the movement of drawing it as a tremendously powerful upward stroke, backhand. You hit your adversary over his right hip and sliced him through up to his left collarbone as the stroke continued on its way. It sounds extraordinary, but it's true. There are so many reliable accounts that we must accept them. There are plenty of men alive now who have seen Japanese officers take prisoners' heads off in one stroke with their swords; and once in the 1939-1945 war a Japanese officer cut through the barrel of a machine-gun in one blow.

There are, of course, skeletons up and down Europe showing how sword or axe severed their arms or legs or ribs or heads. Skulls cut almost in two, or with great slices taken out; thigh bones cut through as clean as a whistle; there was a skeleton found in Gothland with both legs cut clean off below the knee with one stroke. And so on. We have to accept that there is a lot of truth in these stories of enormous blows, just as there is plenty of imagination as well.

Most of the warriors of Northern Europe fought on foot shoulder-to-shoulder behind their shields, forming what they called 'the shield-wall'. This was quite different from the wild rushing tactics of the Franks or the massed charges on horseback of the Goths and Longobards. Sometimes they would form the wall in line, provided that both ends of the line (the flanks) were covered by some natural feature such as thick scrub, or a river, or a lake or the seashore, or a cliff, so that their opponents couldn't get round the ends of the line and take them in the rear. On open moors or heaths they formed the shield-wall as a square or a ring (we often read of 'the shield-ring' or 'the shield-burgh'); and sometimes, when they fought in line with their flanks protected, they used what they called the 'swine-array', that is with a sort of snout out in front. Right in front would be one man, a great champion picked for his strength and valour; behind him would be two others; at their back, four, then eight, and so on. Once battle was fairly joined, however, any formation would break up into lots of single fights. This is well described in the tale of the battle of Bravoll in Sweden.

This was a big battle for those days (round about the year 700) and was fought out between a very aged King of Sweden, Harald Hilditonn (War-Tooth) and his nephew Sigurd Hring.

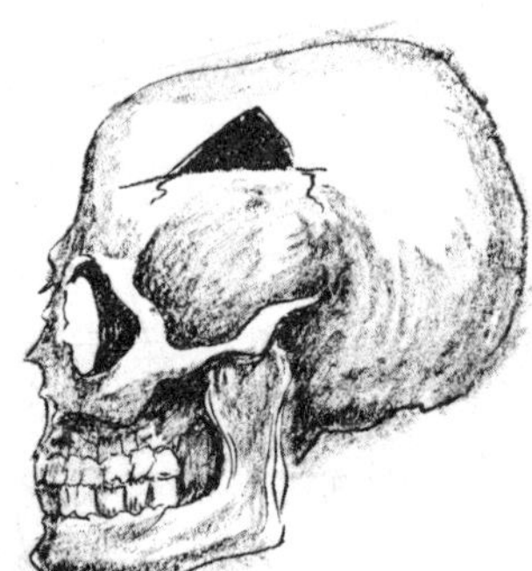

Sword work

It was a battle for the throne, for Hring's folk thought that Harald was far too old, as he couldn't walk. First they tried to get rid of him by smothering him in his tub while he was having a bath, but he asked them, with great dignity, to stop. 'I know you think I'm too old. You're quite right, but I would rather die my fated death; I don't want to be smothered in a bath-tub. I'll die in a much more kingly way.' They agreed, and let his people take him out. Then Hring—who already ruled over half of Harald's realm—agreed that they should fight it out.

'Hring gathered men from all Sweden and Western Gautland and many from Norway; and there were men from Thelemark, whom nobody wanted to have; they were great archers, but were thought to be of little use. When he reached a place called Bravik his ship-host met him, and he camped on Bravoll near the forest, between it and the bay.

King Harald gathered men from all Denmark, and a great host came from Austrriki (*modern Poland, probably*), and all the way from Koenugard (*Kiev*) and Saxland (*the coastal lands of North-west Germany, Schleswig and Holstein*). He sent Herlief with his Saxon force to King Hring in order to stake out the field chosen for the battle.

With Harald were his skalds and champions, and his guard, and there were the shield-maidens Visma and Heid, each of whom had come with a strong force. Vebjorg, another shield-maiden, had come with her men from Gothland in the South.

Many Wends were in Visma's force; they were easily recognized, for they had long swords and bucklers, but not long shields like the other men. On one wing was Heid with her standard, and one hundred champions; these were her Beserks, and many chiefs were there too. On the other wing was Haki Hoggvinkinni (*whose name meant 'Scarface'*) and the standards were carried in front of him.

Harald was in a waggon, for he was not able to fight on foot in the battle. He sent Bruni and Heid to see how Hring had arrayed his host, and if he was ready for battle. Bruni said: "It seems to me that Hring and his host are ready; but he has arrayed them in a strange way; he has drawn up his men in a swine-array, and it will not be easy to fight against him." It was as Bruni had told. Hring had arrayed his men in wedge-shape, so the array looked all the deeper for this; nevertheless it was so broad that one flank reached to the river Vata, and the other to Bravik.

When these hosts were ready for battle, both had the horns sounded, and raised the war-cry. The arrays met, and the battle was so severe, that it is said in all old Sagas that no battle in the Northern lands was ever fought with so many and so valiant picked men. When it had raged a little while, Ubbi the Frisian, a champion, advanced in front of the host of Harald, and attacked the snout of the array of Hring, and first of all Rognvald; their fight was very hard, and terrible blows could be seen in the host where these dauntless champions rushed at each other, dealing many and heavy cuts. Ubbi was such a great champion that he did not cease until their single fight ended by Rognvald's fall; then he rushed at Tryggvi, and gave him his death wound. When the sons of Alrek saw his appalling rush into the host, they went against him; but he was so hardy and skilled that he slew them both; then he killed Yngvi; and rushed so furiously into the ranks that everyone fled before him; he slew all who were foremost in the snout, except those who were fighting other champions.

When Hring saw this, he urged the host not to let one man overcome all, such proud men as they were. He shouted: "Where is Storkud, who till now always has borne the highest shield?" Storkud answered: "We have enough to do, Sir, but we will try to gain a victory if we can, though where Ubbi is, a man may be fully tried." At the urging of the king he rushed to the front against

Ubbi, and there was a great fight between them with heavy blows, as each of them was fearless. After a while Storkud gave him a large wound, and himself received six, all of them severe, and he thought he had rarely been so hard pushed by a single man. As the arrays were dense they were torn from each other, and so their hand-to-hand fight ended. Then Ubbi slew the champion Agnar, and cleared a path in front of himself, dealing blows on both hands; his arms were bloody up to his shoulders; thereupon he attacked the Thelemarkians. When they saw him they said: "Now we need not go elsewhere, but let us shoot arrows at this man for a while, and little as everybody thinks of us let us do the more, and show that we are valiant men." The most skilled of the Thelemarkians began to shoot at him, namely Hadd the Hard, and Hroald Toe; these men were such excellent archers that they shot twenty-four arrows into his breast; this much was needed to destroy his life. These men slew him, but not before he had slain six champions and severely wounded eleven others, and killed sixteen Swedes and Goths who stood in the front of the ranks. Vebjorg, shield-maiden, made hard onsets on the Swedes and Goths; she attacked the champion Soknarsoti; she had accustomed herself so well to the use of helmet, coat of mail and sword, that she was one of the foremost in *Riddaraskap*★; she dealt the champion heavy blows and attacked him for a long while, and with a blow at his cheek cut through his jaw and chin. He put his beard into his mouth, and bit it thus holding up his chin. She performed many great feats. A little after Thorke the Stubborn, a champion of Hring, met her, and they fiercely attacked each other; finally she fell with many wounds and great courage.

Great events happened here in a short time; and first one, then the other array got the better; many a man from both hosts never

★A word meaning, 'all the fighting skills'. In the thirteenth century it would be called 'chivalry'.

returned home, or was maimed. Storkud then made an attack on the Danes, and on the champion Hun, and at last slew him, and a little after one who tried to revenge his death, by name Ella. Then he attacked Borgar, and after a hard fight slew him. Storkud rushed through the ranks with a drawn sword and killed one after another; he cut down Hjort; whereupon Visma, shield-maiden, who carried the standard of Harald, met him. Storkud made a fierce attack on her. She said to him: "The ferocity foreshadowing death is upon you, so you shall die now, scum!" He answered: "All the same, you shall drop Harald's standard first!" and he cut off her left hand.

Then Brai, Saekalf's father, tried to avenge her, but Storkud pierced him with his sword. In the host in many places could now be seen large heaps of slain and fallen men. A little after Gnepja, a great champion, attacked Storkud; they fought hard, and Storkud gave him his death-wound. Afterwards he slew Haki, but received many large wounds himself; he was cut on the neck at his shoulders so that one could see into his chest, and on his breast he had a large wound so that his lungs were hanging out, and he had lost one finger on his right hand. When Harald saw that so many of his guard and champions fell, he rose on his knees and took two saxes, whipped fast forward the horse which drew the waggon, and thrust the saxes with both hands and slew many a man with his hands, though he was not able to walk or sit on horseback. The battle went on thus for a while, and the king performed many great deeds. Towards the end of the battle Harald Hilditonn was struck on the head with a club, so that his skull was broken; and that was his death-wound, and Bruni slew him. When Hring saw the waggon of Harald empty, he knew that he had fallen; he had the horns blown and shouted that the host should stop. When the Danes became aware of this the battle ceased and Hring offered truce to the entire host of King Harald, which all accepted.'

This is a straightforward account of the fight, hard-boiled and not exaggerated, and there are several points worth following up. Harald, for example, had his skalds with him as well as his champions. A skald was a very important member of this warrior society, for he was the poet who sang afterwards of the battle and the great deeds of the warriors. He had to be there, in the thick of it; he had to know what it was like to do great deeds, and to be wounded, so he had to be a warrior too. Most skalds were well-known, so nobody would, if they could help it, kill them, for they sang of the deeds of foes as well as of friends, and you would be daft to kill the poet who could make your name immortal. He was not just a singer, or a teller of tales. He was part war-correspondent, part poet. It is as if a modern war-correspondent was also a great poet, and instead of recording his dispatches or writing them, he sang them in person. We have to remember that there were really very few people in those days; on Bravik there were probably only a few hundred warriors engaged, though it was counted as a great battle. The normal would be seventy or eighty men a side. So almost every warrior knew every other warrior.

Here is a case of the 'swine-array' in action. You'll notice that Hring's line was secured on the flanks by a river on one side and the beach on the other. Then, in the list of the warriors who came to fight (I've shortened it, leaving out all the names of champions) what about the shield-maidens? These formidable girls were a regular feature of Norse life, the earthly counterpart of Odin's maidens, the Valkyrs, the choosers of the slain, who rode invisible over the battle picking out suitable candidates for Valhalla, the warriors' paradise.

In the force of Visma, the Wends (from the eastern shores of the Baltic) carried round shields, 'not long shields like other men'. This is one of the few times long shields are mentioned; a long shield covers a man better (after all, he's long, not round) but a round one has advantages aboard ship, or when you're travelling on foot through forests with it slung on your back, when it will be far less of an encumbrance than a long one.

The whole story is full of names, of course, because it was first told by skalds who were there, and put everybody in. When, centuries later, the story was written down, the names were still remembered; and after all, they were the ancestors of the people who eventually read it. Besides, they sound so splendid! Can you wonder they loved to hear them! Thorkel the Pig-headed, Erling the Snake, Egil Squint-eye, Rognvald the Tall, Odd the Far-travelling, Saxi the Plunderer, Hrolf the Woman-loving, Glismak the Good, Ivar the Boneless, Dag Fat-man, and so on.

We needn't be surprised, either, that these names of heroes and champions were remembered. We have our own heroes from the same period of history: Arthur and Bedivere, Lancelot, Kay, Gareth, Gawain, hosts of them. And aren't we completely at home with Robin and Little John, Tuck the Friar, and Will Scarlet? Even the Sheriff of Nottingham. No other Sheriff, even Bill Hickock, is so well remembered.

The most puzzling thing, perhaps, in this story is that Herlief was sent to stake out the field chosen for the battle. This is because they treated formal battles like duels; and for duelling they had rules and formalities every bit as strict as in the eighteenth century.

You remember Kormac, who borrowed Skeggi's sword to fight a duel? In his saga we are told much about the rules of duelling. First a place for the fight is chosen, and the 'field' marked out with hazel poles at the four corners of a square. So much was this marking out with hazels a part of formal fights, that a battle field was often referred to as a 'Hazelled Field'.

Inside the hazels, a rug five ells (2.286 metres or a bit over 7 ft) square is pegged down. This is set inside a second square, and that is inside a third, and that is inside a fourth, growing successively larger: these three outer squares are marked out so that the gap between one square and the next is 0.30 of a metre (about a foot) wide. The hazels are put at the corners of the outermost square. Each combatant has a 'second' with three spare shields. Each strikes in turn, defending himself with a shield; when all three shields are hacked to pieces, they must stand on the rug and use their swords alone. If either was wounded so that blood fell on the rug, he need not fight any longer. If either put a foot outside the outer (hazelled) square, he was held to have retreated; if he put both feet outside, he had run away. In some cases a man who had stepped off the field could be compelled to come back and finish the fight. The one who ran, or got most wounds, had to pay a fine to his opponent.

Sometimes the field wasn't laid out so carefully:

'There was a fine field not far from the sea, where the Holmganga was to be. There the place was marked out by a ring of stones. Ljot came thither with his men, prepared for the Holmganga with shield and sword. He was very large and strong, and when he arrived on the field at the Holmganga place the Berserk frenzy came upon him, and he howled fiercely and bit the rim of his shield.

Egil made ready for the Holmganga, having his old shield, with his sword Nadr girt to his side and with Dragvandil (*his other sword*) in his hand. He went inside the marks of the duelling place (*i.e., the outer squares marked out round the rug*) but Ljot was not ready. Egil raised his sword and sang.

After the song Ljot came forward and pronounced the laws of the Holmganga, that whoever stepped outside the stones which are set around the place of Holmganga should ever afterwards be called Nithing (*coward*).

Then they rushed at each other, and Egil struck at Ljot, who covered himself with his shield while Egil dealt blow after blow so that Ljot could not strike back. He drew back to get room to swing his sword, but Egil went just as fast after him and smote most violently. Ljot went out beyond the markstones and to and fro on the field. Thus went the first attack. Then Ljot asked to be allowed to rest, which Egil granted.

Egil bade Ljot make himself ready: "I want this fought out," he said. Ljot sprang to his feet, and Egil ran forward and at once struck him; he went so close that Ljot stepped back, and his shield did not cover him. Then Egil smote him above the knee, and cut off his leg. Ljot fell, and at once died.'

Egil's fierce onset was not, according to the rules of Holmganga, fair; for the combatants should swap blows—first one striking, then the other in a fairly orderly way.

'For of old, in the ordering of combat, men did not try to exchange their blows thick and fast, but there was a pause, and a definite succession in striking, the contest being carried on with few strokes, but those terrible; so that honour was paid more to the mightiness than to the number of the blows.'

This is a comment by a late historian, Saxo the Dane, writing in the twelfth century of events of the seventh.

Incidentally, it is interesting to consider the word 'swap'. Nowadays, it means simply an exchange of one thing for another, though in the country a small sharp sickle for cutting grass and nettles is still called a swap, and swapping is the act of cutting the stuff, because of the noise it makes; 'swap, swap, swap' goes the little blade through the stems. That's the noise a sword makes too, as it sings through the air. So, in a duel, you swap blows.

But what about 'the Berserk frenzy came upon him'? This

was a very real thing, and we still use the word today more or less with its original meaning, though we pronounce it wrongly: 'Buzzerk' instead of 'Bare Sark'. Some fighters found it was very effective to give no thought at all to defence, but to give all their force and energy to attack. They did it 'Bare Sark', too—without a shirt, literally; that is, a mail shirt. Going into the fight stripped to the waist, without a helmet, they used to work themselves up into a battle-frenzy before they began to fight. They did actually gnaw the rims of their shields, and howl, and jump up and down. Don't many modern wrestlers and boxers do the same sort of thing? In a lesser degree, of course; but if you want to work yourself up into a violent 'state' where you feel you can tackle anybody, try biting and gnawing at something, and 'going berserk'. It makes a formidable fighter. The real secret, of course, is complete disregard for your own safety. If you *show* that you don't give a damn whether you're killed or hurt, or not, you'll find the other fellow isn't keen to take you on. In the Northern lands in those days many men were professional berserks; professional thugs or bullies really, for their whole purpose was to intimidate more peaceable folk, and to obtain money and other things with menaces.

Without a weapon, a man was no more than a thrall, not complete in the sight of Odin. It was an ancient custom, older than Rome, that a woman brought arms to her man when she married, and it was often women who handed on the family sword or sax as heirlooms. The Roman historian Tacitus, writing long before the migrations began, has much to say about the importance of arms to the German tribes which caused so much trouble to Rome.

'No business, public or private is transacted except in arms. But it is the rule that no one shall take up his arms until the State has attested that he is likely to make good. When that time comes, one of the chiefs, or the father or a kinsman, equips the young warrior with a spear and shield in the public council.'

And again, speaking of council meetings:

'. . . if they approve, they clash their spears. No form of approval can carry more honour than praise expressed by arms.'

Here indeed we can see the germs of the mediaeval idea of the making of a knight, as well as the great importance of arms to all men, in peace not war. Then we read:

'On the field of battle it is a disgrace to the chief to be surpassed in valour by his companions (*companions here being used in the sense of personal following*) or to the companions not to come up in valour to their chief. As for leaving the battle alive after your chief has fallen, *that* means lifelong infamy and shame. To defend and protect him, to put down one's own acts of herosim to his credit, that is what they really mean by allegiance.

The chiefs fight for victory, the companions for their chief. Many noble youths, if the land of their birth is stagnating in a protracted peace, deliberately seek out other tribes where some war is afoot. The Germans have no taste for peace; renown is easier won among perils, and you cannot maintain a large body of companions except by violence and war.

The companions are prodigal in their demands on the generosity of their chiefs; it is always "Give me that warhorse" or "Give me that bloody and victorious spear". As for meals with their plentiful, if homely, fare, they count simply as pay. Such open-handedness must have war and plunder to feed it. You will find it harder to persuade a German to plough the land and await its annual produce with patience than to challenge a foe and earn the prize of wounds. He thinks it spiritless and slack to gain by sweat what he can buy with blood.'

During the period of the Migrations, the weapons of ordinary warriors were spear, axe and knife. The long sax and the sword were the weapons of chiefs; that is why practically every sword of this time which has been found has been of rare and costly quality, richly adorned with gold, silver and jewels. Later, in the age of the Viking sea-raiders, swords became much more plentiful, and though many which have been found are beautifully decorated, they are not so rich as their predecessors; and there are very many whose hilts are of plain iron, though their blades are magnificent. Somewhere around A.D. 850 blade-making entered a new phase, and pattern-welding, that long and costly process, was no longer necessary. Weland's successors could make fine quality blades far more cheaply, so there were many more swords to go round; and because of this use of simpler methods of forging, and better steel, blades were bigger. It is the swords of Vikings which you are more likely to see, and you will find that many of them are extremely well preserved, some looking as if they could still be used; indeed, they could. Many are still nearly as sharp as they used to be.

There is nothing odd, or scientifically impossible, about a sword taken from a grave being used again, good as new, centuries after its burial. You have heard about Skofnung; here's as remarkable a history of the sword Hneitir given to a

Prince of Norway named Olaf when he was given his name; the sword had been taken from the grave of a much earlier King Olaf, but it was taken from his mound to be given to his descendant. This boy became King of Norway in 1015, and was called Olaf the Holy. He fell in the battle of Stiklestad in 1030; as he got his death-wound, Hneitir fell from his hand and was picked up by a Swedish warrior.

> 'He had broken his sword, and he took up Hneitir and fought with it. He got away back to Sweden and kept the sword all his life and his son after him, and so on after another of his kinsmen took it, and always it followed that he who possessed the sword told the next its name, and whence it came.'

A descendant of this man went to Constantinople to join the Emperor's guard, the Varangians, but he found that every night the sword went from under his pillow and was found some distance away. The Emperor heard of this, and offered to buy the sword for three times its worth in gold when he heard to whom it had belonged. So he bought it, and put it above the altar in St. Olaf's church in Constantinople. This story was told by the poet Einar Skulason in Trondheim cathedral in 1153.

Always the poet and the sword. These men valued words, the words of hard courage and fierce poetry. Faced with death, these warriors had a way of using memorable phrases which are not forgotten. These words were a man's memorial, and must be thought out and clearly spoken. King Ragnar Lodbrok (Hairybreeks), son of Sigurd Hring of Sweden, raided in England and was captured by King Aella of Mercia. He was thrown into a pit full of adders, and as he died he said, 'If my piglets knew how the old boar was suffering, they'd grunt to some purpose.' They did: Aella was killed in battle soon after by one of the piglets, Ivar the Boneless, who came to get revenge for his father

When Harald Hardrada, King of Norway, fell at Stamford Bridge in battle with the last king of Saxon England, Harold, in 1066, he asked one of his men to pull out the arrow-head which had laid him low. The man pulled it out. Harald said, 'Let me see it.' The man wiped the blood off and gave it to the king as he lay dying. 'Hm. The man who made this knew his job,' he said.

There is yet another poem made in the eleventh century, telling of the destruction of a big Saxon army by a Danish raiding force at Maldon in Essex. Two lines of it sum up the whole of these Norsemen's code:

Thought the harder, Heart the bolder,
Mood the more, as our might lessens.

This is the age of heroes, some real, some perhaps legendary. Within the span of this five hundred years we meet with Arthur; with Sigurd Fafnisbani, the dragon-slayer whom the Germans call Siegfried; with Clovis, first King of France, and Cadwalader of Wales; with Geiseric the Vandal, Theodoric the Goth, Attila the Scourge of God, Belisarius the noble Roman, who fought the Goths and broke the Empire of the Vandals, and with Charlemagne. It is the misty borderland of history where fact and legend mingle; but with the rich material left for us in the earth we are able to come close to the very life of the great folk-legends of western Europe; if we are still we can almost hear their voices—Sigurd, Charlemagne and Arthur.

No amount of written history can ever compare with the feel in your hand of a sword which may have rung upon the helm of Arthur in that last, dim battle in the West, or of an axe which may have cleft the painted shield of Sigurd.

CHAPTER 6

THE WARRIOR'S DESCENDANTS

IT IS A strange thing that the Roman military machine, so efficient in armament and organisation, should have had no influence at all upon the arms and tactics of the medieval knight. This is even more curious when we consider that the whole civilisation and culture of the Middle Ages, religion, law, literature and art, was based upon Roman practice. But the knight fought exactly as his Gothic or Lombardic ancestor had fought, and his arms were those of the Dark Age warrior, improved and modified. The Roman legionary and his superb equipment vanished as if they had never been.

It is easy to imagine that at some point in time the Dark Ages stopped and the Middle Ages began, but of course it wasn't like that. The change-over from the Classical Age of the Ancient World to the Middle Ages took place very very slowly, it needed some two centuries of slow change to transform one into the other, though certain events hastened the process and marked the occasion. We are often led to believe that the Middle Ages began on a damp October afternoon on a hillside near Hastings in 1066, though in fact two hundred and sixty-six years before, on Christmas Day, A.D. 800, another event took place which laid the foundation of modern, let alone medieval, Europe—the crowning in Rome of Charlemagne as Emperor. No. It is best to assume that at some time between A.D. 500 and A.D. 600 the last vestiges of ancient civilisation had died out in

Europe and a new era had begun. For us in Britain it could be said that our Middle Ages began with the death of Arthur in about A.D. 530, but the ancient world lived on longer here than in the rest of Europe; and it is European, not British, politics, culture and art which form the background to the study of the medieval knight. The Dark Age warrior was his ancestor and pattern, and the ideal of chivalry which ruled his life with its insistence upon the value and sanctity of arms stemmed directly from the old Celtic and Teutonic warrior codes.

Without a weapon, a man was no more than a thrall, worthless to Odin—or to the Lord Jesus, if he was a Christian.

APPENDIX

HOW YOU CAN MAKE A HELMET, SHIELD AND SWORD

IT IS NOT nearly so difficult as you might think to make very effective reproductions of the armour and weapons at which we have been looking, so I will give you a few hints as to how it can be done, based on the practical experience of having done it myself.

There are three ways in which you can make these things. The first is fairly simple and you can do it at home or in a classroom to produce articles which will look splendid, but may not wear very long; the second is really an elaboration of the first to give you something more durable; but if you use the third method, you would almost be making real things, and would need proper workshops for metalworking and woodwork.

We will take each main group of arms in turn—helmets, shields and weapons—and see how to set about making them in each of the three ways.

HELMETS

During the period of the Migrations, as we have seen, there were two main types of helmet, one very scarce (the Sutton Hoo visored type) and one very common (the conical nut-shaped helmet). The making of either type presents the same basic problem: you have to make the skull or bowl of the helmet. There are three ways:

1 mould it in papier mâché (layers of newspaper and polycell paste);
2 mould it in fibre-glass;
3 build it up in strips of card.

You can, of course, make it of metal, either beating it out of one piece or building it up in sections; but this would need a forge, or at least welding equipment.

For methods 1 and 2 you need something to use as a matrix on which to mould your helmet-bowl. The **Sutton Hoo** type has a deep, rounded bowl (the other sort has a taller, pointed one) and if you can get a large enough lump of Multiplas you can model a solid helmet shape in it. Although you could do this with modelling clay, you couldn't work your paper or fibre-glass on it until it was dry and hard, and it would probably crack and break up as it dried, so clay is no good. You might use part of a large rubber ball as a matrix, or even (for paper work) a balloon! You may be able to think of something else, too.

If you can model your matrix in Multiplas, you can model the crest which runs across the top of the helmet as well; if you have to use a ball or a balloon, you'll have to model the crest separately on to the finished bowl.

Once you have got your matrix, prepare plenty of thin paper torn into pieces roughly 150 mm (6 in.) square. You will do best if you have one pile of newspaper and one of white kitchen paper. And mix up a good basinful of Polycell paper-hanger's paste, mixed fairly stiff.

Now smear your matrix well with Vaseline, and you can begin. Get seven or eight pieces of your newspaper, and make them all very wet with your paste. The best way to do this is to spread the paste with your fingers. Messy, but far the best way in the end. Then cover the surface of your matrix with the pasted paper. Now prepare in the same way a batch of pieces of your *white* paper; by putting on alternate layers of newspaper and white paper you can see that you have covered the entire surface, leaving no gaps. Now continue building the thing up with layer after layer until you have at least seven. You will do better to go on until you have ten layers, as you are going to wear your helmet, and will want it good and stiff. When you have put on enough paper, set it aside to dry.

Now while the bowl is drying you can make the cheek-pieces and the neck-guard. These can be cut out of card, and then covered with layers of Polycell and paper. This will make them stiff and hard to match the bowl.

When the bowl is dry enough, lift it off the matrix and trim up the lower edge, binding it with carefully cut strips of paper to make it neat.

The crest can be put on now, made first of rolled-up pasted paper, then strengthened and built up into correct shape. The little boar-heads at the ends can be modelled in pasted paper, or if you prefer, in a suitable modelling compound. The moulded eyebrows can be made in the same way.

Now you have all the main parts of your helmet, except for the visor which you can build up as you did the cheek-pieces, cutting it carefully out in card first and then strengthening it with layers of paste and paper.

The neck-guard in these helmets was fixed solidly to the back, so you can stick yours firmly to the bowl. Use one of the impact adhesives, like Thixofix, or you'll have a lot of trouble holding the pieces together while the glue dries. Your neck-guard should be curved to fit inside the rim of the helmet bowl; allow about 15 mm ($\frac{1}{2}$ in.) of it to go up inside to enable you to stick it firmly.

The cheek-pieces and visor should be hinged to the rim of the bowl. Bore a series of holes in the rim where these parts are to go, with corresponding holes in the upper edges of the visor and cheek-pieces. They can be fastened with a loop of wire through each pair of holes, or by threading a piece of twine through like a boot-lace.

By this time your helmet will be ready to be finished off with whatever decoration you want. If you wish to have the same sort of thing as in the surviving Swedish helmets, you will want to prepare some rectangular plates with figures and patterns in relief. These can be made out of paper or card, and the patterns can either be embossed or drawn on them. Prepare the patterns first, then stick them on with Thixofix or Copydex or Marvin. The ribbon-like strips which divide the plates can be cut from paper, or you can get some of that plastic edging-strip which is made with exactly the right sort of longitudinal ribbing. Cut it carefully to the right size and stick it on.

Now you have to paint it, and a very handsome thing you can make of it. The strips will be gold and the plates silver; the crest will be gold with ribs of silver, so will the moustache and eyebrows, with the red garnets set underneath the eye-brows and round the lower lip. (The Swedish-found helmets shown on pages 29 and 32 do not have the garnets, only the silver plating and the gilding.) But you need not follow this exactly. You can make the plates gilt and the strips silvered, and so on, or you can make the whole thing look like bronze.

A **conical helmet** can be made in the same way. Although it's taller and more pointed than the Sutton Hoo type, you can use a pudding-basin for the matrix. Find one which is the right size—that is, just a bit big for your head (remember the lining has to go inside the helmet), put it down on a board or a newspaper and smear it with Vaseline. But of course it won't have a conical pointed top! You'll have to build this up yourself on the bottom of the upturned basin; it will be easy enough to do this and to complete the shape with a lump of Multiplas or clay—you can use clay for this as such a small piece isn't so likely to break up.

The bowl can now be made just as the other kind would be, with layers of paste and paper, but you will have to take care to get the pointed top nice and neat. When it's dry, lift it off the basin and press the sides at the bottom together a little so that your helmet-bowl is slightly oval. After all, your head is not formed in an accurate circle like the rim of a basin.

You can fit cheek-pieces to this or not, as you prefer; some had them, some didn't. The Frankish helmet from the grave at Morken (page 36) was decorated and strengthened by reinforcing pieces, as you can see. These you can cut from card and stick on if you want.

You can use exactly the same process with fibre-glass, using the fibre-glass mat instead of paper and the catalyst instead of Polycell paste. The result will be a much more durable and strong helmet.

The third method, building the bowl up in strips, is more complicated and will take longer, but doesn't need anything for a matrix. What you will need is several sheets of good tough paper; card is too thick and cracks too easily, and ordinary paper such as cartridge, or sugar or cover paper is too soft. A good, fairly heavy water-colour paper is the best, which you can get at any good art-shop. And the best sort of adhesive is one of the resin ones, like Evostik. You will need also some gesso powder. This may be harder to get, but a good supplier of artists' materials should have it.

For a Sutton Hoo helmet bowl, you begin by cutting a strip of your paper about 40 mm ($1\frac{1}{2}$ in.) deep, and long enough to fit round your head just above your ears, leaving about 25 mm (1 in.) overlap to stick it together. Out of this you make a brow-band to start building your helmet on. It is not a bad idea to make a double thickness of this.

Now cut another strip to make the top of the 'frame'. Stick one end to the inside of the brow-band at the front; curve the strip over as if across the top of your head to the back, making the height and curve that you want; and stick the other end to the inside of the brow-band at the back.

When that is done, you can build up a complete frame by fixing shorter strips to the sides.

Now, note: as I said, this sort of frame is for a Sutton Hoo type of bowl. Not a pointed one. For a pointed one, you only need a brow-band and a lot of triangular pieces, about 50 mm (2 in.) wide at the base, which you stick inside the brow-band and join together at the top.

When your frame, whatever shape it is, is finished you can cover it over criss-cross with strips of adhesive packing tape, to make a solid skin over the frame.

When this is done, your bowl will be more or less complete but will probably look a bit lumpy. This is where the gesso comes in. It is a white powder, made of plaster-of-paris mixed with glue, and when it's mixed with water it makes a stiff creamy paste which dries very hard. Painters used to apply a layer of gesso when they painted on boards, for it makes a beautiful smooth, hard surface which takes paint particularly well. So if you make a good stiff mix of gesso and slap it on to your helmet with a knife-blade it will fill in the dents and cover the lumps and wrinkles. You can smooth it out like the icing on a cake while it's wet, and when it's dry you can smooth and polish it with glasspaper or a file.

Neck and cheek-pieces can be made as before, but should be covered with gesso to match the rest of the helmet.

SHIELD

It is much easier to make a shield than a helmet, though here too there can be a problem—to make it curve. However, it can be done, if needed, though many shields were quite flat.

There are really only two ways you can make a shield, and the only major difference is in the materials you use. You remember that these shields were made of thin boards, dowelled together at the edges, covered with linen or cloth in layers and faced with leather. The best—really the only—way to make them is to follow the ancient method. If you just want very thin, light ones which look more or less right you could make them with the paper-and-paste method, but they would be very fragile.

Let's suppose you are going to use cardboard. What you will really need is strawboard, that tough gingery-brown cardboard which is often used for packing. The soft stuff of grocery cartons is no use as it is too thin. If you can get a big enough sheet of strawboard, you can cut your shield out of it in one piece. (You will want a circle of about 350 to 500 mm or 13 to 20 in. in diameter.) If you can't, use several pieces laid side by side, with your second layer stuck on lying cross-ways to the first. And stick them together with Thixofix, not a water-based glue, for you will need to soak your strawboards if you want a curved shield.

Wet them until they are wet right through, but don't let them get too soggy; then in some sand make a shallow depression to fit your shield. (You *can* do it in the ground, but that is a bit messy.) Lay your wet shield over the depression and press it in; it will tend to straighten itself out, so you'll need to put some fairly heavy weights in it to hold it down. When it dries, it should be the shape you want.

When it is quite dry, glue it all over and stick on a piece of cloth—a bit of an old sheet, or a shirt, or part of a dress—anything you can get; then do the same again. When you've put two layers on the front, put two on the back in the same way.

At this stage, before you put the final facing on the front, you will need to fasten in the straps by which to hold the shield. You will want one to put your arm through about half-way between the left-hand edge of the shield and the centre, and another shorter one about the same distance to the right of the centre. You should use leather straps about 13 mm ($\frac{1}{2}$ in.) broad; the arm-loop should be some 250 to 300 mm (10 to 12 in.) long and the hand-grip about 150 to 180 mm (6 to $7\frac{1}{2}$ in.). They should be placed on the inside of the shield, as I have shown in the drawing. To fix them, bore holes in the right places in the shield and in the ends of the straps; they should be riveted, and boat-builders' copper rivets and washers are about the best things to use. Small nuts and bolts would do quite well, or you could use aluminium household rivets.

When the straps are fixed, put your facing on so that the

heads of the rivets or bolts are covered up. This facing should be of leather, but you may find it hard to get a big enough piece; a good piece of cloth, or even of felt, would serve.

When all this is done, you will find that the edges are very untidy; you can neaten them by using gesso on them, or even Polyfilla, though this will easily chip and flake off. The best way is to use a strip of paper, as shown in the drawing below: about 20 mm ($\frac{3}{4}$ in.) wide with its edges cut into a series of triangular notches some 5 mm ($\frac{1}{4}$ in.) deep. Glue this well and stick it firmly over the whole edge.

Now you can leave your shield like this, and paint it, or

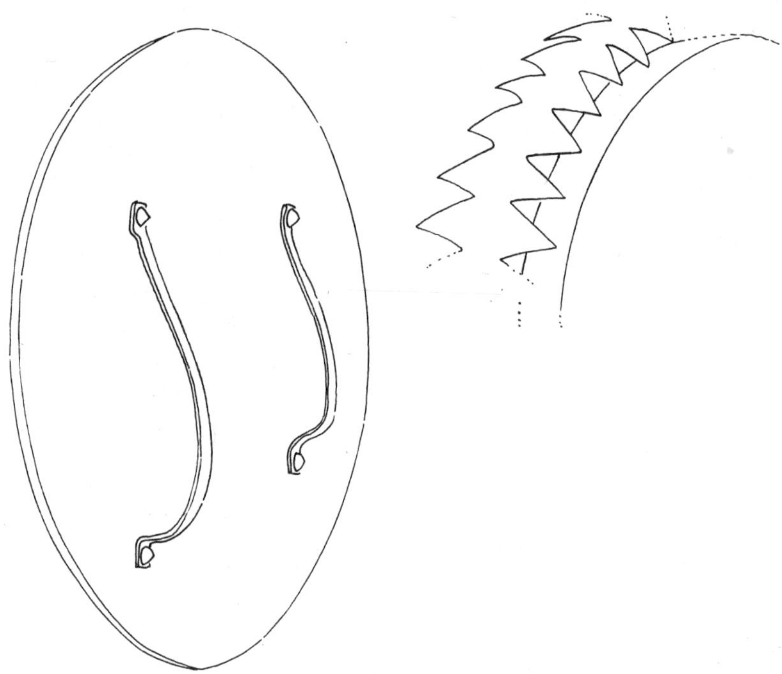

further embellish it with a central boss and applied reinforcing pieces. You can make the boss in the same paper-and-paste way as you made the helmet-bowl, and stick it on; and the reinforcing pieces can be cut out of card.

If you make a real shield, you proceed in the same way, using boards of lime or beech-wood about 3 mm ($\frac{1}{10}$ in.) thick instead of cardboard. You will have much more trouble in bending them to a convex shape, though; you would probably need to steam them, and in my experience you would need a vast amount of steam, playing on the boards for a long time. Apart from this, you would carry on in the same way, but with one difference. To make a shield like the Sutton Hoo one, you should cut a hole in the centre of the boards about 100 mm (4 in.) in diameter, and a corresponding hole in each piece of cloth you stick on to the back or front of the boards.

When you have done this, and put on all your cloth layers, fix in just one strap, the arm-loop on the left of the shield. Then put on your facing. If you have gone to the trouble of using proper boards, go to the trouble of getting a good piece of leather for it, too. This also should have a hole.

Now make your boss, and if you can, beat one out of brass or copper or mild steel. The shape will be the same as in the drawings. For your hand-grip, get a brass or mild steel rod 450 mm (16 in.) long and about 10 mm ($\frac{1}{2}$ in.) in diameter. Leave a length in the centre, corresponding with the diameter of the central hole, and beat the extremities quite flat, and bore a hole in each end.

Fix your boss over the hole now, screwing, riveting or bolting it to the boards with screws or rivets or bolts (about four of them) in the flat rim. Now take your metal bar and fit it to the inside so that its central portion (which is your hand-grip) goes across the hole about 10 mm ($\frac{1}{2}$ in.) to the right of its centre. When you grip this, your knuckles fit inside the hollow boss, as shown.

The decorative reinforcing pieces on the outside can be made from metal, sheet brass or copper, of about 18 gauge for preference. You can really go to town on these, as on the boss, for they can be made very splendidly and can be gilded or enamelled when you have cut and filed them out. You can make your rim of metal, too, though it's a toilsome business; it is easier to make it as I've described for the paper rim, only using leather instead of paper.

WEAPONS

When it comes to making weapons, the methods are much the same; it depends upon what you want. As swords, axes and spear-heads can be made in the same way, I shall only go into detail in the matter of making swords and scabbards.

You can make them of wood, of paper (believe it or not), or of metal. Let's see about wood first.

The important thing in *any* method you use, is not to try and make your sword out of one piece. It will in the long run be far more satisfactory to make it as real ones were made, assembling all the elements of blade and hilt. There will be five main elements: one blade, one lower guard, one grip, one upper guard, and one pommel. Have a look at some of the swords I have drawn in Chapter 3, and decide which kind you want.

(If you choose type 3, there are only two parts to the hilt, for as you can see, guards and grip are made in one.)

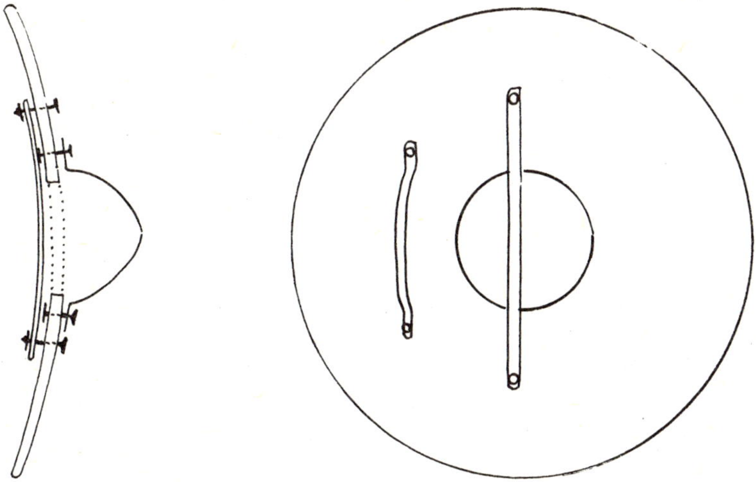

Whatever you use to make your blade, you will probably (like the old swordsmiths themselves) make your hilt of wood, or, if you can, of ivory or bone. This is really very simple; it's just a question of shaping the pieces properly and seeing that they are pierced with openings to fit properly over the tang. It is the blade which sets the problems.

If you carve it out of wood, try and get a good, hard wood with a long grain, and keep the grain running lengthways up and down the blade, not across it. You will need a slat of wood about 850 mm (3 ft) long, 50 mm (2 in.) wide and 6 mm ($\frac{1}{4}$ in.) thick. Look at the drawing. Now cut your wood out to the shape of the blade; from this point you begin to shape it, bevelling off the edges first. When you have done this, begin to thin the whole thing down, getting your slat thinner towards the point. You won't be able to go *much* below your 6 mm ($\frac{1}{4}$ in.) of thickness or you'll get it too weak. The shallow fuller will have to be carefully cut with a gouge, or you can file or sand-paper it out if you prefer.

When you have finished your blade, you can slip the parts of the hilt over its tang, and glue them in place. You can't rivet over the top of the tang as you would if the blade was made of iron.

It is a lot more complicated to make your blade of paper, but it might be worth-while to suggest how. By paper I mean, as before, good quality water-colour paper.

First, cut out two identical pieces the shape of your blade. Don't bother about the tang at this stage. Now take a long ruler—a proper ivory-edged folder is the best thing—and draw a line down each side of your two pieces 6 mm ($\frac{1}{4}$ in.) in from the edge. This defines the edges of your blade. Next, holding your straight edge against each line in turn, bend your paper against it to an angle of about 45 degrees. Now if you put your two pieces face to face, you'll see that you have the beginnings of a blade.

Being just made of paper, it is likely to be flabby and will want stiffening. You can run a length of steel bar down the middle, but wire is easier to come by. The best thing really is to get two long bicycle spokes—for they are very stiff and quite straight—and cut off the fixings at each end.

Now you have your two flat paper pieces of blade, with the sides bent to form your edges, and the two spokes to stiffen it. You will need a tang, and this can be made of a piece of wood

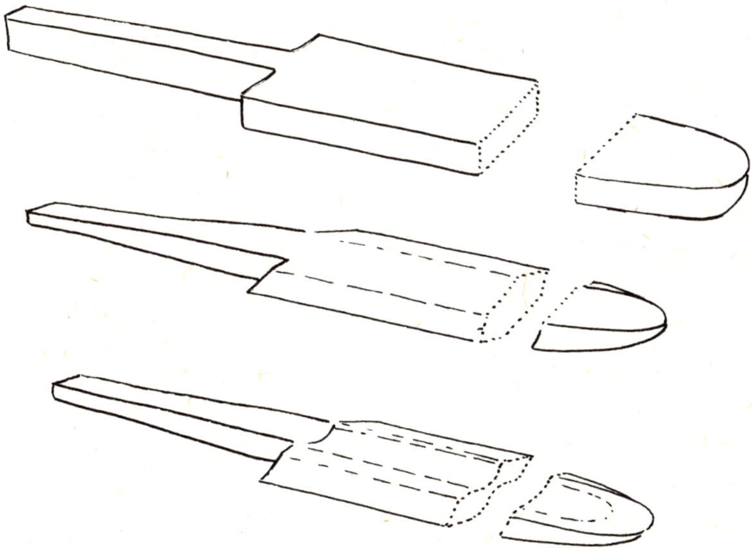

about 150 mm (6 in.) long by 12.5 mm ($\frac{1}{2}$ in.) wide by 6 mm ($\frac{1}{4}$ in.) thick. Shape it so that it tapers toward the top on all four sides to about 6 mm ($\frac{1}{4}$ in.) wide by 3 mm ($\frac{1}{8}$ in.) thick, and flatten the wide, lower end a little.

The whole blade is ready for assembly now, but you can further strengthen it by giving the paper a good coating of shellac varnish. Let it dry, and give it a second coat for good measure; then, when both pieces are *really* dry, cover every bit of their inner sides with Thixofix. Lay one piece flat on the table, its inner, glued side upwards, and put your two spoke-stiffeners—also coated with Thixofix—in the folds of the edges, so that the upper ends come just below the top of the piece. Now lay your tang in place in the dead middle of the top of

I.

the blade, so that about 12.5 mm ($\frac{1}{2}$ in.) of its lower end is on the paper. This is where you have to be careful, for when you put down your other piece of blade on top of the first piece, it will stick fast at once, so it is important to have the point and edges exactly together. Stick your two bits firmly together, pressing the extreme edges close and the middle portion, but taking care not to press down the raised ridges at the edge of the fuller. If you're careful, you'll find that you now have a very convincing-looking blade, and a pretty stiff one too.

The hilt, of course, is treated exactly as in the method described before.

The scabbard can be made in the same way; you can use two *very* thin slats of wood, about 6 mm ($\frac{1}{4}$ in.) broader than your blade, bent and shaped to fit over it, but this is rather difficult. Almost as good is the water-colour paper, and nearly as strong; it's much easier to bend and shape, too; all you have to take care of is that your glue is only on the extreme edges, for if it gets inside the scabbard it may stick your sword in. The whole thing should be covered with a 'skin' of cloth, maybe two or more to stiffen it. This will hold it firmly together and prevent it from coming apart at the edges. Cut your lengths of material so that they will overlap by about 3 mm ($\frac{1}{8}$ in.) straight down the middle of the back of the scabbard. If you want a particularly good-looking scabbard, you can put a finishing cover of leather or velvet over it all.

The mounts can be made of paper, too, but it would be perhaps better, and nearly as simple, to make them of very thick foil or of thin metal.

As for using metal for your sword, it is possible to make a blade which is about as good as an authentic one, but you need a forge and a skilled smith. Sword-blades can be made out of spring-steel, and tempered, to produce a real blade, or out of a good piece of Victorian wrought iron, which would make a very fine imitation of one; but the most possible method is to use aluminium bars in exactly the same way as you would use a slat of wood. You cut it with a saw in the same way, and shape the edges, point and fuller with files instead of with chisels and sandpaper. Many excellent swords are made for films and the theatre in this way.

Maybe I have been able to suggest various ways of doing the more difficult-seeming jobs in making arms, but I think really that once you *want* to make anything, so long as you know what the real original was like, and how it was made, and what it was made of, and how it was put together, you will have no real difficulty in making it, or something remarkably like it, for yourself.

INDEX

An asterisk means that an illustration appears on the relevant page.

NORTH SEA
GOTH
LEAVE H
ABOU
300 B
ANGLES AND SAXONS. RAIDS FROM ABOUT A.D. 240 LARGE SCALE SETTLEMENT FROM A.D. 450
ANGLES & SAXONS
LONGOBARDS A.D. 17
VANDALS EAR
IN FIRST CENTURY A.D
FRANKS A.D. 250 CONFEDERATION OF GERMAN TRIBES
CROSS RHINE A.D. 405-6
CHALON A.D. 451
MIGRATE AFTER A.D. 437. CLOVIS FOUNDS KINGDOM A.D. 481
BURGUNDIAN KINGDOM A.D. 444-534
VISIGOTHIC KINGDOM AFTER A.D. 410-507
VISIGOTHIC KINGDOM AFTER A.D. 410-711
SETTLE A.D. 568
ROME SACKED, ITALY OCCUPIED A.D. 410
HUNS BESIEGE ROME A.D. 451
ANDALUSIA A.D. 409-429
MEDITER
GEISERIC LEADS VANDALS INTO NORTH AFRICA A.D. 429 AND FOUNDS KINGDOM
SEABORNE RAIDS ALL OVER MEDITERRANEAN. ROME SACKED A.D. 455
VANDALS DEFEATED BY BELISARIUS A.D. 533
N
E
S
W